PARANOID, OR SO THEY SAY

PARANOID, OR SO THEY SAY

By

Alex Robinson

Copyright © 1997 by Alex Robinson

All rights reserved. No part of this book may be reproduced, stored in a retrieval system, or transmitted by any means, electronic, mechanical, photocopying, recording, or otherwise, without written permission from the author.

ISBN 1-58500-171-6

About the Book

The Beatles in songs, in epigraph form, create a coordinating theme relating to this story. The book is based on an appeal, a courtroom battle involving innocence, presumption of guilt, perjury, corrupt plaintiffs, including a sick incompetent mom. There is also corrupt Dearborn Heights, Mich. police sworn testimony to the Wayne County, Mich. court authorities and Judges. The plot involves abuse of power in reality. And you wonder how many other UAW, immigrant, ethnics are wrongly convicted.

TABLE OF CONTENTS

	Page
CHAPTER 1 Introduction to Your Friend Paranoid Schizophrenia	1
CHAPTER 2 Trial of the Century	21
CHAPTER 3 Father-Son Mix-up Project at the Mental Hospital	48
CHAPTER 4 Father-Son Mix-up Project at the Probate Court Guardianship	66
CHAPTER 5 Further Tragedy of Magnitude	83
CHAPTER 6 Closing Arguments of a Friend	101

CHAPTER 1

UNITED STATES DISTRICT COURT
EASTERN DISTRICT OF MICHIGAN

Plaintiff, Alex Robinson

v.

Defendants, Anatol Zolkewsky and Myron Zolkewsky

Dearborn Heights Police Department

Civil Action N⁰ 86-75034

Judge, Richard Suhrheinrich

    Your Honor, I am appealing to your Court and to you, in order to overturn and remove my entire record of insanity, to overturn the 14 felony charges of psychopathia and psychosis, to remove the 14 criminal misconduct charges on the case, and to overturn mental incompetency records. These records exist in the Probate Court in the County of Wayne, State of Michigan, on my estate and matters.
    I will base my appellate motion to do the items stated in the above paragraph on the evidence I will provide.

I claim the basis of PERJURY, CONTEMPT OF COURT, and FRAUD against the Courts; PERJURY, CONTEMPT OF COURT, and FRAUD against the Judges; and FRAUD against several government-mandated offices involved in my case.

"Sergeant Pepper's Lonely Hearts Club Band" and "A Little Help From My Friends,"
<u>Sergeant Pepper's Lonely Hearts Club Band</u>, The Beatles.

    I anglicized my name to Alex Robinson from Alexander Zolk, Jr., near Christmas of 1977. I did this to enter a university and chose an anglicized name in my family structure, which would be one set of my grandparents that were here in the U.S.A.[1] My old name at the point of my birth, May 15, 1954, was Alexander Zolk, Jr.[2]

    Now, for the Case Record and the history of items.[3]

    My case started when I was transported to a mental hospital on June 4, 1976.[4] This case is based on the plaintiffs: Dearborn Heights Police Department, individual officers, and Mrs. Caroline Zolkewsky, my mom.

Summary

Affirmed felony charges and criminal misconduct items: Three charges of reckless driving reported to AAA car insurance of defendant, Alex Zolk, Jr., and also reported as driving penalty points, 18 driving points in total, to the Department of State, Michigan Driver's License Section of defendant, Alex Zolk, Jr. Three assaults and batteries on family members, especially the father.

At Preliminary hearing, June 30, 1976, Judge Joseph J. Pernick agreed with the plaintiff.

On July 21, 1976, Judge Frank S. Szymanski ordered the record of insanity, ordered the record of mental incompetency, ordered the incarceration, all based on the six charges. The incarceration occurred at Wayne County Psychiatric Hospital, Westland, Michigan. The judges in the case also agreed with a psychiatrist and his documentation.[5]

I claim as my response a statement from paragraph #2 -- "He fully comprehended the statement and started to ask the examiner to convince his father to drop the petition." I claim this to be my defense.

I will prove PERJURY, CONTEMPT OF COURT, and FRAUD by the Dearborn Heights Police Department, individual officers, and two brothers, Anatol and Myron Zolkewsky, who literally dictated to my crippled mom the above against the Courts; PERJURY, CONTEMPT OF COURT, and FRAUD against the Judges; and FRAUD against several government-mandated offices involved in my case.

In paragraph #4, the provisional specific diagnosis is: "Schizophrenia, paranoid type," based on the violent history as presented by the family.

In paragraph #5, the psychiatrist's findings are the specific conduct of examined person in the recent past that provides the basis for the prediction. I, Alex Robinson, claim as my response a statement from paragraph #5: Even though he is 'denying' all the allegations presented in the petition, I claim this to be my defense on my behalf.

I will prove PERJURY, CONTEMPT OF COURT, and FRAUD, these by the Dearborn Heights Police Department, individual officers and two brothers, Anatol and Myron Zolkewsky, who dictated to my crippled mom the above, against the Courts; PERJURY, CONTEMPT OF COURT, and FRAUD against the Judges; and FRAUD against several government-mandated offices involved in my case.

Let us start on the documents,[6] and there are documents,[7] with paragraph #1, "plaintiffs respectfully represent to the court the allegations." Paragraph #2, "I further represent that the facts upon which the allegations of mental illness or mental retardation are based are as follows, and are of my own personal knowledge except as to those facts stated to be upon information and belief."

The defendant, Alex Zolk, Jr., from the court petitions, "totaled three cars - lost insurance on cars - [and] did bodily injury to father and brothers."

Hence, this relates to the affirmation of three charges of reckless driving and three charges of assault and battery upon my father and brothers, this in regards to the plaintiffs in the case, the Dearborn Heights Police Department, individual officers, and two brothers, Anatol and Myron Zolkewsky, who dictated to my crippled mom.

I state that these six felony charges, these six charges of criminal misconduct, are false statements. There is no evidence to support these allegations now or 10 years ago.

I claim PERJURY, CONTEMPT OF COURT, and FRAUD, these by the Dearborn Heights Police Department, individual officers and two brothers, Anatol and Myron Zolkewsky, who dictated to my crippled mom the above against the Courts; PERJURY, CONTEMPT OF COURT, and FRAUD against the Judges; and FRAUD against several government-mandated offices involved in my case.

Further from paragraph #3: I further represent that I believe the individual should be admitted by petition only. And, from paragraph #5: I further represent that my basis for knowledge of the individual's condition is [the subject's] mother. From paragraph #6: I further represent that the names . . . of any witnesses with personal knowledge of any of the alleged facts are (the) Dearborn Heights Police [and] brothers. Paragraph #7: I further represent that the names and addresses of the individual's parents, his closest living relative, and other persons I believe would be interested in the proceedings and outcome following this petition for individual's commitment are as follows:

Interested Parties

Name | Relationship to Individual
Zolkewsky's | Family
Dearborn Heights Police | Officers called to home

Paragraph #9: "I therefore pray that the subject of this petition be admitted by order of said court to a suitable hospital or facility."

Finally, at the end: "I declare under the penalties <u>of perjury</u> that this petition has been examined by me and that the <u>contents thereof</u> are true to the best of my information, knowledge and belief." Dated June 21, 1976, signed Mrs. Caroline Zolkewsky.

In regards to the items from the above document, I claim that the plaintiffs, the Dearborn Heights Police Department individual officers, were: from paragraph #1 - they were disrespectful to the court. From paragraph #2 - they misrepresented all the facts in the matter, and they created misinformation and wrong information. They lied to the medical doctors and lied to the psychiatrist in giving facts about an individual's behavior and problems, that I claim, were nonexistent as data from the M.D.s. From paragraph #7 - they further misrepresented any constructive interest in the proceedings and outcome after the defendant's commitment and incarceration. From paragraph #9 - in their prayers on these court documents they in fact, lied severely; hence the contents thereof are all false testimony on record of the defendant.

I claim PERJURY, CONTEMPT OF COURT, and FRAUD against the Courts, PERJURY CONTEMPT OF COURT, and FRAUD against the Judges, and FRAUD against several government-mandated offices, involved in the case.

Items outline in ink.[8] Present, Honorable Frank S. Szymanski, Judge of Probate: "It appearing to the court, the sworn testimony having been taken in open court in regard to said matter, and after a full investigation as to said matter . . . that there is clear and convincing evidence that the subject of the petition is a person requiring treatment. It is therefore ordered that the individual not be discharged if hospitalized and be admitted to Wayne County Psychiatric Hospital for a period not to exceed 60 days; it appearing to the court from the findings entered on the record that the hospital can provide treatment which is adequate and appropriate to the individual's condition."

I will prove false sworn testimony on this case from the plaintiffs, and from the findings entered on the record in this entire case: I will also prove that the plaintiffs created PERJURY, CONTEMPT OF COURT, and FRAUD in the matter of the defendant, the judge and the court.

From paragraph #2 regarding day treatment in a hospital[9]: "He is . . . depressed . . . he is considered a potential danger to himself and others." From paragraph #4: "He requires 24-hour supervision on a locked ward. His provisional diagnosis is schizophrenia, paranoid type."

I will prove there should have been a more favorable report on Alternative Treatment Programs on my case, I claim that there is PERJURY, CONTEMPT OF COURT, and FRAUD against the Judges and Courts on my case and even the medical doctors.

Items outlined in ink.[10] Present, Honorable Joseph J. Pernick, Judge of Probate: "It is therefore ordered that the individual remain in Wayne County Psychiatric Hospital for custody provided that any period of detention . . . the date of receipt by the court being June 21, 1976."

This is where the problem started in my case, and I am going to prove that there is PERJURY, CONTEMPT OF COURT, and FRAUD upon the Judges, the Court, and the plaintiffs involved in this case. Also, the plaintiffs, Anatol, Myron, and the Dearborn Heights Police Department, created FRAUD upon several government-mandated offices involved in this case.

Items outlined in ink.[11] For the record, the type order "Petition" where the city was "Dearborn Heights, Michigan, 48127;" this was from my Michigan Driver's License Identification that I had on me.[12] The data brought in on the record, I state, is falsified and does not belong there as stated.

I state that I kept my patience in this occurring event where my blood pressure is noted at B/P 110/40.[13] Also, I kept my patience in this occurring event with my pulse 80. Note that under Mental Condition (Delusions, Hallucinations, Illusions) there is no entry, but it was left open for observation later on. Also, under Tendencies (Violent, Depressed, Elated, etc.) there is a line drawn through this category, meaning "negative." Condition of Person (Nutrition, Cleanliness, etc.) noted "clean." Under Quality and Condition of clothing is stated "good." Articles found on person is noted as: wallet, wrist watch, car keys, driving license, and $7.30.

Items outlined in ink.[14] "Unemployed, single, white male, . . . brought in here by police . . . he had an argument with his father today. According to the petition . . . [he] totaled three cars, lost insurance on cars, . . . did bodily injury to father and brother . . .; . . . he had had an argument with his father, who was a 'Ukrainian' immigrant to the U.S., . . . he believes he is controlled by a director of weight lifting training, and his father is chasing him . . . he had worked as an orderly in Ingham Medical Hospital in Lansing for two years. Upon examination, he appears to be in good physical condition and fairly good personal appearance. He was cooperative, . . . verbally productive . . . he was coherent; . . . he was oriented as to times three; . . . his intellectual functioning seemed to be average; . . . . . . Impression: Schizophrenia, paranoid type; disposition; involuntary admission." The examining psychiatrist was B. Ahn, M.D.

I claim that most of these items are true and for the rest of the data to the doctor I will prove PERJURY, CONTEMPT OF COURT, and FRAUD by the plaintiffs in this case.

These are some documented items that are outlined in ink.[15] "[He was] unemployed . . . brought to the hospital by the police as the patient struck his father at home. Apparently the patient has been acting bizarrely for quite some time prior to his admission to this hospital . . .. The situation became worse and the family could no longer tolerate patient's behavior. The patient was hospitalized on an involuntary basis."

I will now summarize my clinical course in the hospital: Physical: "Within normal limits clinically." Laboratory: "Routine CBC, chest x-ray, urinalysis, and serology were all negative." Psychological Testing: "Not referred." Progress in Hospital: ". . . his rather long stay in the hospital." Disposition: "The patient was discharged." Final Diagnosis: "Schizophrenia, paranoid type." Psychiatrist, Eui Yol Cho, M.D. Some of these items are true and some of these items are false testimony. I will prove PERJURY, CONTEMPT OF COURT, and FRAUD by the plaintiffs in this case.

Present medical illness and chief complaint:[16] "The patient does not appear to be ill at this time and complains of no physical ailments." General appearance: "Well." Head: "The head is normocephalic." Eyes: "Pupils are round, equal, and react well to light and accommodation. Conjunctivae are normal." Ears: "Earways are clear and drums are normal." Nose and throat: "No septal deviation. Tongue and throat are clear." Neurological examination: "Reflexes are physiological; no sensory changes; no weakness or paralysis." Impression: "Physical examination within normal limits clinically." Psychiatrist, Eui Yol Cho, M.D.

Some of these items are true, other items are false testimony on this case record.[17] They are outlined in ink. " . . . unemployed, . . . who was brought in by his father . . . with the assistance of police from home. According to reports, patient attacked his father at home. He also, according to these reports, had been acting bizarrely for the past several months prior to his admission . . . . Patient's family on this occasion was able to call the police and have patient brought to this hospital. Patient was hospitalized here on an involuntary basis."

Attitude and general behavior: "He was rather tall and his body build was quite athletic. He was cooperative in the interview; . . . patient was quite anxious and tense during the interview."

Stream of mental activity: "His verbal productivity was within normal limits."

Emotional reaction: "He was extremely cautious, tense, and guarded during the interview. He would become argumentative with the therapist once in a while."

Mental trend, content of thought: "Patient reported he has been unemployed in the past six months and has been looking for a job desperately . . .. He was becoming 'depressed' . . . now and then because of his unemployment. Before his admission, he had had some vodka and he hit his father with his finger when he lost judgment. He would anxiously try to argue with the therapist that it would be wrong to keep him here just 'for one minute's misjudgment out of my 22 years of existence.' He also stated his father had returned from another trip to the Ukraine and was teasing the patient by telling him how he had spent American money behind the Iron Curtain. Patient expressed his anger toward his father, saying he was constantly ridiculed by his generation at the athletic club in college because of his father's repeated trips behind the Iron Curtain."

Sensorium, mental grasp and capacity: "Patient was well oriented as to three spheres. His memory for both recent and remote events appeared to be intact. His intelligence appeared to be slightly above average; . . . his judgment was also quite pathological."

SUMMARY

"This is a 22-year-old, single, unemployed, ex-college student who was brought in by his parents with the assistance of police from home; . . . and on the day of his admission he attacked his father who had returned from another trip to the Ukraine . . .. He was extremely tense and cautious; . . . he was oriented; . . . his memory was intact; . . . his intelligence appeared to be slightly above average."

External stress: "Moderate." Diagnosis: "Schizophrenia, paranoid type." Prognosis: "Fair with continuing psychiatric treatment. Recommendations: 1) Obtain court order to treat the patient." Psychiatrist, Eui Yol Cho, M.D. I will refer to the above document later on in this case concerning my goals to prove that the plaintiffs created PERJURY, CONTEMPT OF COURT, and FRAUD against the Judges, Court and government-mandated offices involved in this case.

Items outlined in ink.[18]

> Informants - the patient's mother, Mrs. Caroline Zolkewsky . . . interviewed by telephone because she could not come to the hospital.
>
> Previous Psychiatric Hospitalization:
> According to the informant, patient was an outpatient at Ingham County Community Services. The patient denies that this information is true.
>
> Factors Precipitating Hospitalization:
> The patient stated that his father had returned from a vacation . . . on 6-20-76, the father was bragging, according to the patient, about the money he had spent on the trip. The patient indicated that he has been unemployed for over six months and he was drinking one hundred proof vodka during his

father's discourse . . . and became enraged that his father had spent so much American money behind the Iron Curtain. The patient stated that he hit his father with his finger.

According to the patient's mother, the father's partial bridge work was loosened and eye blackened.

The patient's mother called the Dearborn Heights Police Department . . . on 6-21-76, the patient's mother filed the petition and the patient was brought to Wayne County Psychiatric Hospital by the Dearborn Heights Police; . . . admitted on an involuntary petition. The mother stated that in 1974, she noticed some bizarre behavior. He claims that his mother spent the money his grandfather left him; . . . spent more than $800.00 in one month. The patient has been enraged that his father travels and spends American money backed by American gold in communist countries. The patient stated that in the . . . his grandfather's death; . . . the patient refers to his father as his 'immigrant father,' meaning that he is not native born. The patient indicated that he did not have any trouble until at the university it was noticed on his records that his father was born in an Iron Curtain country, and upon further investigation, it was learned that he has a passport and traveled there; . . . . The patient attempted on two occasions to have his father's passport revoked. He was told by federal officials to stay out of his father's affairs . . . .

Reportedly, the patient has totaled three cars, ... The mother reports seeing the patient bang his hear repeatedly against a wall or hit his head with his fist or a wooden board.

Pertinent Social History:
The patient's father is 65 years old and is a

naturalized citizen of the United States, having immigrated to this country from the Ukraine after World War II, about thirty years ago . . .. The patient's mother is 50 years old and was born in Michigan.

According to the mother, the patient's father speaks broken English and must have things explained to him in Polish, Ukrainian, and German.

The grandfather showered the patient with gifts and neglected the patient's brother. The patient never developed a close relationship with his father because of the language barrier.

According to the patient's mother, the father is a 'tightwad, passive, and an isolate.' He goes to his workshop in the basement upon arrival from work every evening. The patient's father claims to be too busy in the winter in his workshop . . . a wife's duty to follow her husband's religion and traditions . . . she considers this a mistake now, . . . he attended public school and graduated from the public school system. He was considered a good student . . . he was a member of the . . . football and hockey teams . . .. The patient's grandfather died in 1965, leaving the patient and his brothers a trust fund.

The patient was granted a partial academic scholarship to attend Michigan State University. The patient was involved in . . . weight lifting . . .. He worked as an attendant at the Ingham County Hospital . . . partial science scholarship in pre-medicine at the Lyman Briggs School at MSU.

Current Family Structure, Living Arrangement, and Relationships:
 . . . lack of money for tuition. He registered at

Wayne State University, but did not attend. The patient is now living at home with his parents. His maternal grandmother, age 82, now lives with the family . . .. The patient took a bartender's course and worked as a bartender at Mr. Ed's Bar for six months . . .. The patient is presently unemployed and has no income. He is supported by his father who works at Ford Motor Company with an annual income of $17,000.00.

Identified Problems:
. . . 2) unmet dependency needs; 3) feelings of inferiority and insecurity because of his ethnic background; . . . 5) poor father-son relationship with feelings of rejection.

Diagnostic Impression:
. . . and always been embarrassed by his father's lack of skill with the English language. The patient's grandfather was a kind, nurturing role model . . .. The patient felt inferior on the university campus, because of his ethnic background . . .

. . . The patient has become overzealous in his feelings of patriotism to overcome his ethnic background.

Casework Focus and Discharge Plans:
. . . The patient will be discharged to his parents' home when maximum inpatient service has been received . . .

The patient was adamant in his denial of the allegations of bizarre behavior made against him in the petition to hospitalize him involuntarily.[19] . . . He refused, when given the opportunity, to sign a voluntary petition, stating that he wanted it on record that he was in the facility forcibly . . .. After the patient's preliminary hearing on 6-30-76, . . . mentally disturbed, . . . the judge state that he had to go to court on 7-21-76. At his final hearing he was ordered hospitalized . . .

. . . to help the patient become independent and be responsible for his actions and decisions . . .

. . . He was brought to Wayne County Psychiatric Hospital by the Dearborn Heights Police Department on 6-21-76 on a court petition filed by his parents . . .[20]

. . . The patient had been displaying bizarre behavior for more than two years . . . his final hearing on 7-21-76 . . . .. It is suspected that the patient had been ill for some time, but it is impossible with the data given to determine when the patient became ill . . .

. . . developed no insights into the causes of his illness . . . .. His father had 10 years of college training in law and had served as a judge in the Ukraine before the Russians took over the country . . .

Also, he disclosed that he has always felt inferior because of his ethnic and "blue collar class" background . . .

Reportedly, his mood was depressed, his skills were below average . . . .. He was referred to the Educational Service . . . he was not given any tests to determine his level of functioning . . .

It was reported that the patient stated he did not wish to waste his time on fictional material. Further, he was not certain he understood fiction . . .

Patient Affairs Department. He went to that office and learned that he might be eligible for Social Security benefits . . .. The patient applied for Medicare . . .. He explained that he would have to sell his car because he could no longer afford to pay the cost of insurance . . .. The patient was referred to Vocational Rehabilitation . . .. He appeared to be motivated to train for productive employment; however, he was not certain of the areas in which he was most qualified . . .. He stated that he would depend on the counselor and the DVR evaluation to guide him in making his decision . . . that his decision to become a doctor had been unrealistic . . .

He stated that his father had made regular visits to see him and they had established a more positive relationship . . .. He was pleasant and cooperative . . .. The patient came to this caseworker's office on the day of his discharge to thank this caseworker for the interest and effort on his behalf. He expressed confidence in himself to manage his future . . .

"Don't Let Me Down," Hey Jude, The Beatles.

The patient was discharged on 8-27-76, and will return for aftercare with Dr. Cho every two weeks. The accomplishment of the casework focus is evidenced by the patient's decision to become involved in a training program. It is the consensus of Dr. Cho and this social worker that psychotherapy with the doctor is the most feasible treatment at this time.

I state that some of the items from the above documents are true, and other statements are false testimony by the Dearborn Heights Police Department individual officers and the plaintiffs in the case, so far, Anatol and Myron Zolkewsky.

I will prove that the plaintiffs made PERJURY, CONTEMPT OF COURT, and FRAUD against the Courts, the Judges, the doctors, and their staff. I will prove that the plaintiffs made FRAUD against several government-mandated offices in response to my case.

ENDNOTES CHAPTER 1

1. Document: Change of Name, Wayne County Probate.
2. Document: Certified Copy of Record of Birth, Wayne County Courthouse.
3. Documents: State of Michigan, Probate Court for the County of Wayne, in the Matter of Alexander Zolkewsky, Jr., the Application for Admission by Medical Certification and Petition for Admission and corresponding documents, filed June 21, 1976.
4. Document: Order of Examination and Transport, all three paragraphs, ordered by Judge of Probate, Willis F. Ward, dated June 21, 1976.
5. Document: Physician's Certificate dated June 22, 1976, attached to the aforementioned court documents, The Psychiatrist: Eui Yol Cho, M.D.
6. Documents: Westland Medical Center, Medical Record Inquiry Response, regarding my case number and the entire corresponding documents and attachments from the copies of court documents, other documents, and the psychiatric records from my patient charts. These start with my Admission Record on June 21, 1976 in Wayne County Psychiatric Hospital.
7. Documents: Outlined in ink, Psychiatric record copy from the State of Michigan, Probate Court for the County of Wayne in the Matter of Alexander Zolk, Jr., Application for Admission by Medical Certification, Petition for Admission, this dated in upper left corner, June 4, 1976.
8. Document: State of Michigan, Probate Court for the County of Wayne, in the Matter of Alexander Zolk, Jr., Order following hearing on petition, dated July 21, 1976.
9. Document: State of Michigan, Probate Court for the County of Wayne in the Matter of Alexander Zolk, Jr., report on Alternative Treatment Programs and Evaluation of Adequacy of Treatment, provided by the hospital, dated July 9, 1976.

Psychiatrist, Su Jin Chung, M.D.

10. Document: State of Michigan, Probate Court for the County of Wayne in the Matter of Alex Zolk, Jr., the Order following preliminary hearing, dated June 30, 1976.

11. Documents: Westland Medical Center, Medical Record Inquiry Response regarding my case number and the entire corresponding documents and attachments from the copies of court documents, other documents, and the psychiatric records from my patient charts. These starting with Admission Record on June 21, 1976 in Wayne County Psychiatric Hospital.

12. Document: Admission Record, Alex Zolk, Jr., dated June 21, 1976, for W.C.P.H.

13. Document: Admission Record to Ward D-401 dated June 21, 1976.

14. Document: Wayne County General Hospital, psychiatric consultation dated June 21, 1976.

15. Document: Wayne County General Hospital Record Report, Discharge Summary. Date of Admission: June 21, 1976 and Date of Discharge: August 27, 1976, signed by the psychiatrist and dated September 30, 1976.

16. Document: Wayne County General Hospital physical examination dated June 25, 1976.

17. Document: Wayne County General Hospital, dated August 20, 1976, Alex Zolk, Jr., Mental Examination.

18. Document: Wayne County General Hospital Record Report, Alex Zolk, Jr., dated June 24, 1976, Page #1.

19. Same Document - Progress Note August 4, 1976, by social work intern, Josephine Lampton.

20. Same Document - Progress & Suspension Note, August 30, 1976.

CHAPTER 2

Caroline Zolkewsky having been first duly sworn by the Court Clerk to testify, testified as follows:[1]
Caroline Zolkewsky Direct Examination:
[Wayne County Prosecutor]: Who is Alex Zolk, Jr.?

Mrs. Zolkewsky: He is my son.

[Wayne County Prosecutor]: You signed the petition on the 21st of June of this year?

Mrs. Zolkewsky: Yes.

[Wayne County Prosecutor]: To obtain the petition?

Mrs. Zolkewsky: Well, my son has been ill since the latter part of 1973.

[Wayne County Prosecutor]: When did you sign the petition?

Mrs. Zolkewsky: On June 20th.

* * *

[Wayne County Prosecutor]: Did he make any threats at that time?

Mrs. Zolkewsky: Not at that time.

[Wayne County Prosecutor]: Did he threaten to hit anyone?

Mrs. Zolkewsky: No. I resumed our conversation.

[Wayne County Prosecutor]: At any time during the period did he threaten you or anyone else?

Mrs. Zolkewsky: Not at that time.

[Wayne County Prosecutor]: Did he after that time?

Mrs. Zolkewsky: Yes.

[Wayne County Prosecutor]: Let's talk about the time when he threatened someone.

Mrs. Zolkewsky: My husband stepped into the house and immediately my son went over to him. By the time I reached my husband, his face was a pool of blood and blood was on his shirt, and I got the operator and she called the police.

Cross Examination:
[Attorney Dennis James]: You indicated he never had an argument about this before.

Mrs. Zolkewsky: Before?

[Attorney Dennis James]: You never discussed it before?

Mrs. Zolkewsky: Yes, but there was not any problems.

*   *   *

[Attorney Dennis James]: Your husband went out of the door?

Mrs. Zolkewsky: Yes.

[Attorney Dennis James]: Hurt?

Mrs. Zolkewsky: On the face.

[Attorney Dennis James]: A bloody nose?

Mrs. Zolkewsky: Not only a bloody nose, he also--there were four or five teeth that were damaged, and he cannot chew or eat presently.

[Attorney Dennis James]: You called the police?

Mrs. Zolkewsky: Yes.

[Attorney Dennis James]: Did the police issue a warrant?

Mrs. Zolkewsky: No.

*   *   *

E. Cho, M.D., having been first duly sworn by the Court Clerk to testify, testified as follows:

[Wayne County Prosecutor]: What is your diagnosis?

Dr. Cho: Schizophrenia, paranoid type.

[Wayne County Prosecutor]: Is that a mental illness?

Dr. Cho: Yes.

[Wayne County Prosecutor]: Upon what do you base your diagnosis?

Dr. Cho: Upon my first examination. This is defensive behavior . . . [which] made me able to form a diagnosis at the first examination . . . . I would not specify how he would be harmful to himself.

[Wayne County Prosecutor]: Is he harmful to others?

Dr. Cho: Yes.

*   *   *

[Wayne County Prosecutor]: Did you understand her to say that her son chased the father out of the house and harmed him?

Dr. Cho: Yes.

[Wayne County Prosecutor]: But you do think he is harmful to others?

Dr. Cho: Yes.

Cross Examination:
[Attorney Dennis James]: Doctor, you indicated two examinations of Mr. Zolk, Jr.?

Dr. Cho: I said or mentioned two examinations, but I did have a lot of examinations.

[Attorney Dennis James]: You indicated that he did not give what you would consider normal responses to certain questions?

Dr. Cho: He was quite tense. The only information I could get from him was that he was a little bit drunk the day before admission, and he hit his father with his fingertips. He said he hit his father with his fingertips, and for that reason he was at the hospital, that this would be a terrible mistake to keep a person in a psychiatric hospital for one minor misjudgment.

[Attorney Dennis James]: [Is] that not an ordinary response to your question?

Dr. Cho: Not at all.

"Hey Bulldog," <u>Yellow Submarine</u>, The Beatles.

Alex Zolk, Jr., having been first duly sworn by the Court Clerk to testify, testified as follows:

Direct Examination:
[Attorney Dennis James]: What is your current occupation?

Mr. Zolk: I am unemployed.

[Attorney Dennis James]: Where did you last work?

Mr. Zolk: On I-75 at a place called Mr. Ed's. I have no present income.

[Attorney Dennis James]: How far did you get in school?

Mr. Zolk: I am a pre-med student and I have 117 credits.

[Attorney Dennis James]: Were you planning to return to school in the fall?

Mr. Zolk: This fall I was not sure. I have to first allocate my funds, because my parents do not support my education.

* * *

Mr. Zolk: For the purposes of not taking my parents'

income, we had the argument. Well, I had been sitting on the couch, reading the paper, since I have been unemployed for a half a year. And my father, who had returned 24 hours, was making fun of me and accusing me of all sorts of things. Accusing me of all sorts of criminal activities.

[Attorney Dennis James]: Did you argue again?
Mr. Zolk: No. After the police were called on me, I stopped the argument.
[Attorney Dennis James]: You said you had some vodka drinks at the time?

Mr. Zolk: Yes.

[Attorney Dennis James]: Do you feel that led you to do something that you might not have done?

Mr. Zolk: I have never argued or struck my father until this time on the 20th of June . . .. It could have been the vodka . . . first of all, I have no funds.

Cross Examination:
[Wayne County Prosecutor]: Why did you hit your father with your fingertips?

Mr. Zolk: Because I could. At Michigan State, your Honor, it is on my record that I have taken computer science courses and received accreditation.

Mrs. Caroline Zolkewsky, having been duly sworn by the Court Clerk to testify, testified as follows:

Rebuttal Examination:
[Wayne County Prosecutor]: In your previous testimony, you testified as to what he did to his father?

Mrs. Zolkewsky: First he chased his father outside.

[Wayne County Prosecutor]: Let me ask you if this was an isolated incident?

Mrs. Zolkewsky: Well, I have two other sons who are 19 and 17.

*   *   *

[Attorney Dennis James]: Your Honor, I think the testimony will show that this was a long-standing dispute in which Alex may have shown poor judgment.

[The Court]: The petition will be granted as prayed.

"Gimme Some Truth," Imagine, John Lennon/Plastic Ono Band (with The Flux Fiddlers).

I will prove that some of the testimony is true and the other testimony items are false statements by the Dearborn Heights Police Department individual officers, and false statements by the plaintiffs, Anatol and Myron Zolkewsky who dictated to my crippled mom, in regards to my case.

I will now provide the evidence to prove PERJURY, CONTEMPT OF COURT, and FRAUD upon the Judges, upon the Courts, and on several government-mandated offices involved in the case.

Your Honor, I am presenting this artist's reconstruction sketch relating to the testimony of the plaintiffs: Mrs. Caroline Zolkewsky, Dearborn Heights Police Department individual officers, and the supposed victim, Alexander Zolkewsky, Sr., my father.

The Order following Hearing on Petition states[2]: "It appearing to the court, the sworn testimony having been taken in open court in regard to said matter, and after a full investigation as to said matter

. . . that there is clear and convincing evidence that the subject of the petition is a person requiring treatment."

According to my admission application[3], I "did bodily injury to father." Hence, this relates to the assault and battery charge upon my dad entered in this court in the County of Wayne, instead of the local City of Dearborn Heights District Court.

Also, a progress report, made by the social work intern, Josephine Lampton, states that[4] "According to the patient's mother, the father's partial bridge work was loosened and eye blackened." "My husband, his face was a pool of blood, and blood was on his shirt[5] . . .. There were four or five teeth that were damaged and he cannot chew or eat presently."

These statements are lies created by the plaintiffs. There is no evidence presented by Dearborn Heights Emergency Medical Services, the ambulances, the paramedics, nor private ambulances, the medics, the Emergency Room registered nurses, or the Emergency Room doctors.

I wrote a letter of request to the City Fire Chief for records concerning this incident[6]. The Fire Department required permission from the city's attorney to release the documents, with the research data given as being true, according to all known facts of the matter stated in my letter of request.

Finally, I received a letter from the Fire Chief, which states[7], "We have researched our records and determined that the fire department did not respond to . . . any medical emergency involving . . . Alexander Zolkewsky, Sr., 8090 Dale, June 20, 1976." But Dr. Cho states that I[8] "was brought in by his father . . . with the assistance of police from home."

I state that there is no evidence from Wayne County General Hospital Emergency Rooms for the above paragraph's items in this case, nor from any other Emergency Rooms in the County of Wayne. Contrary to what the record states, there is no evidence of emergency airway reconstruction of my dad, no emergency blood transfusions, no emergency pain medications, no emergency air suctioning of airways, no emergency suturing, no emergency ophthalmic (eye) surgery, no emergency dental reconstruction, collections of calcium teeth particles did not exist for storage, no maxillary (upper jaw) surgery, no mandibular (lower jaw) surgery, no nasal bone surgery and reconstruction, no plastic surgery, no cosmetic surgery, nor further ophthalmic (eye) surgery, no placement of dentures directly on damaged bones with the removal of broken and damaged and chipped teeth. None of these items in the above paragraphs occurred nor will they ever occur. From the given testimony of the plaintiffs in the case, which I state is PERJURY, FRAUD, and CONTEMPT OF COURT, the above emergency medical procedures and any and all other medical procedures are not presented as evidence in regards to their testimony and in regards to the case.

Also, there is no evidence presented from my father's Blue Cross/Blue Shield Medical and Health Insurance Plans from Ford Motor Co. and the UAW concerning this long matter of surgical and medical rehabilitation concerning the damages of record in this case.

The next document I need to submit as my defense evidence is the photocopy of having a good history on record as being a member of the American Automobile Association, or AAA, Automobile Club of Michigan. I have been a member since 1979, and have dues paid ahead to 1980. Before 1979 and back to 1976, by court order, I did not have a car, nor car insurance, nor car club membership, nor vehicle registration, nor plates on a car, but I did have a valid Michigan Driver's License. From 1970 to 1976, I did have AAA membership and AAA car insurance, which I will present in a while.

The next document that I am presenting is the AAA club membership, which was back in 1976 in my full possession and separate from my AAA car insurance.

I want and need to discuss my situation involving my valid Guaranteed Arrest Bond Certificate. The present one is something like the one I had which was valid ten years ago, in June and July, 1976.

According to my Order of Examination and Transport,[9] "It is therefore ordered that the individual remain in Wayne County Psychiatric Hospital for custody provided that any period of detention . . . the date of receipt by the court being June 21, 1976."

I need to present the evidence of my AAA club membership, somewhat similar to the valid one I had ten years ago, in regards to the Guaranteed Arrest Bond Certificate. It declares for Alex Robinson, present as in the past, that: "Auto Club Group Insurance Company hereby guarantees the appearance of the member whose name and signature are on this card in any court when arrested for any motor vehicle law offense

. . . (except driving under the influence of alcohol or drugs, failure to appear for prior traffic violations, or driving with a suspended or revoked driver's license) committed prior to the membership expiration date shown on the reverse side thereof; and in the event of the failure of said member to appear in court at the time of trial, payment of any fine or forfeiture levied for such failure to appear not in excess of ONE THOUSAND DOLLARS ($1,000) is hereby guaranteed.

"All public officers are hereby authorized and requested to

accept this certificate in lieu of other bail. The member agrees to reimburse the Guarantor for payments it makes pursuant to this Bond Certificate."

On June 30, 1976, I requested release on bail bond certificate and arrest bond certificate, with my valid AAA club membership from the judge in the above preliminary hearing. I have tried, but I cannot obtain the transcripts to that specific preliminary hearing. I state that for the record.

Since I was accused with my supposed third charge of reckless driving just recently by the plaintiffs, Anatol and Myron Zolkewsky who dictated to my crippled mom, and the Dearborn Heights Police Department individual officers, I felt that I had the right to place my certificate to the judge. The judge refused my certificate and detained me in the Psychiatric Hospital, June 30, 1976.

The documents that I am presenting now, a booklet, forms my next basis of defense. It is the Safety, Boy Scouts of America, Merit Badge Series. A basic theme, on the cover, reads: "The one in the mirror is the one responsible for YOUR SAFETY. FIRST."

On page 2, there are the requirements for the merit badge. My counselor was a police detective, in a sharp business suit, in the Dearborn Heights Police Department. He was a merit badge counselor for our Troop 1145, Our Lady of Grace Church, located in Dearborn Heights. I have not seen him since about 1968, but I understand he is now Lieutenant Detective Richard MacIntyre, still in the Dearborn Heights Police Department.

In my case starting in 1976, I utilized whatever data I could remember in order to discuss items with my defense attorney at that time, of these events that did occur upon me.

My next document to present in behalf of my defense is my membership in the National Eagle Scout Association, started back in 1969. I will prove that I have been perjured upon in this court of law, for the past ten years on my case by the plaintiffs. I feel that I received good legal counsel, good guidance, and proper support from the college association that I am a member of, but because of my court problems I could not be more actively involved in any service that was part of the association.

For the next documents in my defense, I present "*You and the Law*" by Reader's Digest, from the Henry Ford Centennial Library, Dearborn, Michigan. I used something similar to this for my Safety Merit Badge grading when I was a teenager.

I present Chapter Four, "Your Protection Against Crime and Criminal Charges." And note the chapter epigraph by William O. Douglas: "It is better, so the Fourth Amendment teaches, that the guilty sometimes go free than that the citizens be subject to easy arrest."

Note the following definitions from *You and the Law:*

Assault and Battery: "An assault is an open threat of bodily contact with someone; the actual contact is a battery . . . which are felonies" (15B).

Reckless Driving: "If you are guilty of violating a traffic ordinance, you are generally charged with an infraction. If you fail to meet a standard of care that is imposed on you by statute, you will be charged with reckless driving, a violation which is usually defined as 'willful and wanton disregard for the safety of persons and property'" (261).

Collision Insurance: "Provides funds for damage to your car resulting from a collision or from overturning" (287).

Financial Responsibility Laws: "More than half the states have mandatory insurance laws, which require you to obtain minimum liability insurance for bodily injury and property damage before you can register your car . . .. In any state failure to possess adequate liability insurance or to post the bond after an accident will result in the suspension of your driver's license for as long as three years" (288).

Cancellation of Your Insurance: "The company generally may not cancel the policy unless you fail to pay the premiums of your auto registration or diver's license . . . has been suspended. The company may also cancel your policy if it discovers that you obtained the policy fraudulently - by not disclosing prior accidents, for example. In any event it must give you notice of cancellation and, in most states, tell you the reason" (294).

Licenses to Drive: "No one may legally drive a motor vehicle anywhere in the United States without carrying in his possession a driver's or operator's license issued to him by his state of residence" (251).

Local Traffic Ordinances and Driving Regulation: "Driving laws and regulations may be enacted by states, counties, townships and municipalities" (260).

Basic Things You Should Know About Criminal Procedure: "Considering the importance of a criminal trial to the accused person, no one accused of a crime should defend himself without the assistance of a qualified attorney who knows this particular field of law. The Court System: The state courts exist side by side with the federal courts but are concerned largely with offenses against the state constitutions and statues enacted by the state legislatures" (173).

Criminal Charges: "Conviction for the commission of a crime is not only a matter of establishing that the crime was committed as charged . . . but there is a wide assortment of defenses available to persons charged with crimes under certain circumstances" (164).

Insanity: "Mental disease . . . to the charge of commission of a crime, in such cases the tendency across the country is not to sentence such a person to prison but to commit him to a mental institution where he will receive treatment until the authorities running the institution believe he has been sufficiently cured to be allowed to return to society" (168-9).

If You Acted in Self-Defense: "In defending yourself, other people and your own property, you are entitled to use non-deadly force to whatever extent the circumstances warrant" (172).

I state these items for the defense appeal in the court, and I will revert to some of these items in a while concerning my knowledge, behavior, and actions up to 1976.

The plaintiffs and the prosecution have presented their version and any evidence to support their case upon me as the defendant. Now I will explain the basis of my behavior and actions on June 20, 1976, and even occurrences that took place afterward.

First of all, I made a defense statement, sheets of paper with pencil printing on them, and handed them to the doctors and the staff, as well as to my defense attorney. I was not allowed to do them in ink.

I was not handed copies in ink of my defense statements which my attorney and I gave to the doctors and the staff, then in 1976, nor presently in 1986, when I requested my entire case record from the storage facilities located in Wayne County. So, I feel that the defense statements that I made were thrown out, probably in late July, 1976, because they were just pencil and paper items, not for findings of case record.

I state that I did not assault or injure my father, Alexander Zolkewsky, Sr., as is testified to in this case. He received no permanent injuries, nor immediate injuries, when I poked him with my finger in his forehead. I feel he was more in the wrong in this minor incident, and feel I have proved it.

Also, if I remember correctly, back in September, 1976, my father was commenting to my grandmother, Janina Robinson, that he was seeing a dentist for work on his dentures. I had overheard this conversation.

Through comments made by the plaintiffs and the individual officers of the Dearborn Heights Police Department, I know that my father had dentures put in him. I claim this was not due to me and his bodily injury which I did not cause, but that the dentist's treatment program was to remove embedded teeth and to put in standard dentures as proper dental procedure. This was not due to bodily injury, as stated on my court records. This was due to his old age and old, embedded teeth that were removed by a dentist during that time period.

My driving record clearly shows no three charges affirmed of reckless driving from 1980 to 1986. For some reason, I could not obtain my records from May 1970 to 1979 from the Department of State.

So, I make this statement: I do not have from May, 1970, to June, 1976, three charges affirmed of reckless driving, nor six points multiplied by three separate acts for a supposed total of 18 points, on my driver's license record during the time period of May, 1970, to June, 1976. Also, I did not have three separate court appearances regarding the above items, anywhere in the State of Michigan, nor any fines paid to any court jurisdiction in the State of Michigan, concerning the above matters.

Hence, from August, 1974, until April, 1985, on the 1972

Mercury discussed, it was in operating condition with my dad and myself in the family and it was safely driven, licensed, and thus, it had the proper insurance coverage mandatory for vehicles in the State of Michigan.

I tried to obtain the official record from the Department of State concerning the vehicles I owned from 1981 back to 1970, but I could not obtain the documents I would need to show the proper items of license and plate registration, vehicle types of registration, and title record on the vehicles.[10] I would have needed these to show to the court that when I sold the vehicles to purchasers, I basically released all ownership from the vehicles and also basically transferred my auto insurance.

I state that I did not have three reckless driving acts, nor did I destroy three of my cars while driving, nor did I receive six points multiplied in three separate acts, nor did I pay court costs nor fines, nor have to pay any towing charges because of my actions in my cars, nor is there any police reports to obtain associated with any driving records.

I have owned the following vehicles, which are listed from most recent back to age 16:[11]

1971 Ford Custom 4 door, from June 1975 to September 1975

1964 Ford Galaxy 2 door, from October 1974 to June 1975

1968 Buick Electra 225-4 door, from September 1974 to October 1974

1964 Ford 2 door, from May 1970 to February 1972, period of high school

Again, I stress I could not obtain proper documents regarding the above items to show that I did not do what the plaintiffs have affirmed on the case record.

But I will now begin to show valid documents from other sources which pertain to my case and concern items which will show that the plaintiffs are lying to the courts and the judges as well.

I present additional data to the court and the judges in the form of more Automobile Insurance Policies from my AAA Club Membership functions, in order to present as to the actions of the plaintiffs and my father concerning the period of time in this case. I cannot explain their actions concerning the above documents. These are dated from July 22, 1974 up to October 27, 1976, with policy term to May 19, 1977.

Now I state that I did not commit three acts of reckless driving, based upon the evidence which I presented to the court. I did not commit three acts of reckless driving with loss of my car insurances each of these times, supposedly in the period between 1974 and 1976.

Now I would like to present additional evidence pertaining to this case, with explanations and data for the persons involved, including myself, with hopeful results.

My progress report from the hospital states:[12] "According to the mother, the patient's father speaks broken English and must have things explained to him in Polish, Ukrainian, and German; . . .. According to the patient's mother, the father is a tightwad, passive and isolate. He goes to his workshop in the basement upon arrival from work every evening. The patient's father claims to be too busy in the winter in his workshop . . . a wife's duty is to follow her husband's religion and traditions . . . she considers this a mistake now."

My psychiatrist and the staff stated that I was to have placed upon me a record of mental incompetence, a record of insanity, a record of brain damage and disease to be treated according to the case.

In conclusion, the psychiatrist and the staff, from the plaintiffs, are stating that I was unrealistic in coming from a "blue collar class" background, a poor economic background, and yet going into high-technology academic studies on a university level.

The doctors' staff felt it was bizarre and unrealistic behavior for me to work in academics, I could not find my Michigan State University Student Identification to state to them that I was allowed to be a "poor blue collar class" student involved in "high-tech" studies in any university. The psychiatrist refused to even mention the above program, but I did not have my MSU Student ID to begin the discussion, so I stated that one of the plaintiffs removed my MSU Student ID before it could be verified by the doctors and the staff.

In high school I took a college preparatory program as my counselor told me that I might not be able to obtain employment in my father's Ford Motor Co. Rouge Steel Plant. So my dad and my counselor, who was a University of Michigan alumni, both helped me to prepare in pre-college education and planning as I finished in high school.

We basically took this course because there was not much employment available to me at that period of time, and additional education and training was advised by my counselor and my father.

I received a letter from Senator Plawecki, which stated,[13] "I would like to congratulate you on your achievement in the Michigan Competitive Scholarship Test . . . Congratulations again on your Scholarship Award." I received some financial aid in my post high school education and training for employment, whereby a college degree in the sciences or the high technology field was allowed to be an attainable goal by my dad, supposedly with my mother's consent. Also, I was accepted to Michigan State University in a pre-medicine program, where the selection committees knew of my minimal funding and unsupportive parents. But my father did agree that I should accept the partial scholarship offering from the State of Michigan.

I could not obtain from MSU the documents to show the financial aid which I received from my freshman to early junior year during the time period discussed.[14] So, I will state and place these items in the record of my case investigation on this matter.

" . . . 1972 to 1973 . . . Academic Year . . . $700.00;
Summer 1973 . . . $400.00;
. . . 1973 to 1974 . . . Academic Year . . . $900.00;
. . . Total . . . $2,000.00;"[15]

I accepted and fulfilled a partial scholarship program.

I was involved in a Work-Study and Tutoring program in pre-medicine studies with night shift orderly job duties for a period of over two years under the realm of doctors and nurses.[16]

Note that I was employed from December 1972 until February 1974, when I was asked to be terminated with no real reason given.

But later on, in June 1974, I was asked by the professors in my pre-medicine program at MSU to apply to be rehired at Ingham Medical Hospital from June 1974 until I finished my program in February 1975. I finished my pre-medicine minor and tutoring program in the Spring 1975 term, and then transferred. I state the above items for the case.

I present this evidence of my minor in pre-medicine studies, allowed by the University, obtained by partial scholarship, Work-Study and Tutoring, and my father's and mother's and my college trust fund, as I chose the fund to be placed with my dad's permission, and then I even transferred to our home area.[17] This college trust fund was established by my grandfather, Carl Robinson, for this purpose and was to be spent by the age of 21 years of age by me, or it would become income tax payments to the IRS.

Note in Spring 1974, when I lost my job in the hospital, I also failed most of my university courses. I somehow related both areas, but I was given no answer by the authorities and the Lyman Briggs School, as well as the hospital, why this was related.

I state now that maybe the plaintiffs, especially Mrs. Caroline Zolkewsky, was somehow involved in this mishap, as I term it. Because the very next term I was allowed to repeat the failed courses in the Fall of 1974 with passing grades and I was even rehired at the hospital job.

Finally, my pre-medicine minor grade point average was 3.0, with my overall GPA a little lower, when I transferred in the Summer of 1975 to my home area. I could not obtain additional scholarships, could not find a steady summer job in the campus area, and my total funds were low, so I decided to just look for employment in the Metro Detroit area. My father refused to offer me a job in his factory, or maybe there just weren't any openings, and he did not want to co-sign any student loans around the Michigan area, and he did not want to co-sign an equity loan on family property which was free of liability and no mortgages on the family assets.

I felt that I still did the right move, going from high school and accepting any financial aid, and completing a high-technology field of study coming from a low-income household.

My progress report from June 24, 1976, states: "He believes he is controlled by a director of weight lifting training, and his father is chasing him."[18] For June 24, it states, "The patient has become overzealous in his feelings of patriotism to overcome his ethnic background."

The above items area a focus of the record of incompetence, record of insanity, a mental illness to a severe degree based on the facts given.

I now support my statements ten years ago with the following evidence: ". . . Fred Lowe, and MSU graduate, is a two-time Olympian and will be trying out for the weight lifting team in the 165-pound weight class . . ."[19] and "Fred Lowe, a 1970 graduate of MSU, has qualified for a spot on the United States Olympic weight lifting team . . ."[20]

With the above items, this is what I was talking about concerning the problems I had with a father not ever involved in my school sports programs. Nevertheless, I got involved as a college weight lifter on an amateur basis, with donations to the MSU Weight Lifting Club during my period on campus. These donations in turn helped my tutoring in this field and were part of the funding of the Olympian athlete that I was in the same club with, as I was finishing my academic studies at MSU, and finishing my college weight lifting also at that time.

Since I did not have my MSU Student ID at the time, I could not prove that this was good behavior, that there was PERJURY, FRAUD, and CONTEMPT OF COURT upon me that day, June 30, 1976, when a reference to the Olympian athlete who was accepted by the United States Olympic Committee to Team USA, was chosen. I could not obtain permission to seek him out by letters or telegrams for a proper character comment from the MSU campus, concerning my good behavior in his area of the club, and the local community rules and regulations of which I was charged with violating traffic and criminal and civil laws over the period of years on the campus and even in the home area. This is affirmed by the plaintiffs on the case record.

It seems the plaintiffs and the victim, my father, deem that I must be mentally ill, incompetent, must have a record of insanity, because they seem to affirm that my behavior is not proper concerning the above items for record as well as the following documents. They seem to affirm to the judges that my donations in the past, near past, present and future to the following functions are unacceptable actions to them, and are the basis of psychopathia and incarceration in a psychiatric hospital, according to the plaintiffs.

My father and I, over the last 12 years from 1974, have both been able to have the tax deduction allowed for the above "charitable contributions," and this has been a good part of my college education.[21]

I state that I was in good behavior in working through my Work-Study program in pre-medicine, of which I will show areas of having reference pertaining to my MSU transcripts already presented.[22]

I had a roommate, an MSU grad and banker in Okemos, Michigan, who I shared an apartment with for the Summer of 1974 in East Lansing, Michigan.[23] He directed me with an article from The Wall Street Journal to fully customize a cargo van and to sell it on the new market. I did this in order to salvage my college trust fund money and to complete my minor in pre-medicine at MSU for the following academic year.

DETAILS OF CUSTOMIZING THE CARGO VAN

Hence: Acquisition Cost was $3,600.00

Cargo Van Depreciation for . . . two years . . . because 1975 models were out on the car market, this at 20% usage. So:

$3,600
X   20% Depr./Yr.
$ 720 Depr./Yr.
X   2 Years
$1,440 in depreciation on the orange cargo van

So . . . $3,600
           -1,400 as depreciation expense
           $2,200 as a subtotal

Plus: Customizing Features

My father and mother agreed with my banker roommate on the plan, and I received about $1,000 to invest in the van from the trust fund in July of 1974.

The investment featured:[24] Padded Dash, two white low-back bucket seats, chrome trim on the outside, two size F and two Size L poly tires, also known as racing tires, with four chrome mags as wheels, spare tire mount with tow chain and key lock mounted on the roof, AM-FM Eight Track - Four Channel music system with four speakers that were then mounted in the van, fiberglass insulation throughout the van, carpet padding on the walls and the floor, shag carpeting, thin tapestry on the back windows imported from the Far East Indian continent, and thin tapestry right behind the two bucket seats on a spring drapery rod.

So:$2,200.00 as a subtotal
+1,000.00 for customizing investment
$3,200 as the investment cost and a break-even point.

With this figure of $3,200, I added about ½ the amount for my labor and dad's labor and profit also. This was because of the new experimental market for customized vans in 1974. So, $3,200 plus $1,500 equals the asking price of $4,700.00, priced to sell.

I placed an ad in the paper, and found a gentleman with his girlfriend. They stated $4,700 was way too high. He offered $2,700, and I counter-offered with $3,700. He stated it was a 3-speed manual transmission, with a small slant V-6 engine, hence, he offered $3,000. I counter-offered at $3,200. This was my investment cost and break-even point, so I needed to sell. We shook hands and made a contract, a business deal. My dad also agreed with my decision, later on. So, I sold my customized 1973 Dodge orange van at $3,200.

But, when the Trustee, Caroline Zolkewsky, closed out and canceled the Trust Fund, done in August of 1974, there was what seemed to be a delayed withdrawal concerning the above events in this report that I made.

Mother angrily stated that she took my money and grandmother's money, without our knowledge or approval, and she did the transaction in the Spring of 1973.

When my father told my mother to do the final withdrawal, including the $1,000 to customize my van in July of 1974 she became angry, as usual.

When she gave me the canceled passbook in late September of 1974, I noticed the withdrawal for most of the cost of the van was allocated in late July of 1974, and not in the Spring of 1973, like my mother had said.

She became very angry and said she replaced grandmother's portion of the money used to purchase the van, which was done a year ago. I asked why she did it and why she lied to me and dad. She just got angry and screamed at the both of us.

I feel she committed violations as a trustee-mother, especially in not listening to my statements.

Now the plaintiffs have claimed that I "totaled" my cars. However, this was not the case at all. Take, for example, the case of my 1968 Dodge Charger.[25] It is noted on the record that I explained to the hospital that I would be selling it: "He explained that he would have to sell his car because he could no longer afford to pay the cost of insurance."[26]

If my car was "totaled," how could I have even considered selling it? Next, I'd like to present the classified ad I placed in the *Detroit News* on Sunday, September 5, 1976: "Charger '68. Good cond. Make offer. 565-7907."

Would I have tried to sell a "totaled" car by stating in the newspaper that it is in good condition? Clearly, I was telling the truth to the hospital, and the plaintiffs were lying. I sold a good used car in order to pay bills and to prepare for the future. And I had valid insurance on this car during the year in which I sold it.

I was placed on Social Security Disability Benefits,[27] this by court order, starting in July 1976, with placement upon the court order on work status of non-employment and disabled with record of insanity, affirmed by the plaintiffs.

I was also placed on Medicare by the judge's orders in July 1976, and was not able to obtain my own health and medical insurance because of the court order in 1976, until the present.

Hence, I state that the plaintiffs, Anatol and Myron who dictated to my crippled mom, and the individual officers of the

Dearborn Heights Police Department committed PERJURY and CONTEMPT OF COURT upon Judges and Courts in this case. And the plaintiffs committed FRAUD against several government-mandated offices involved in this case, a few of them being the Social Security Administration, Medicare offices, Michigan Department of Education, Vocational Rehabilitation offices, Michigan Department of State, and AAA Auto Insurance Company of Michigan.

ENDNOTES CHAPTER 2

1. Transcripts: State of Michigan, Probate Court for the County of Wayne, in the Matter of the Estate of: Alex Zolkewsky, Jr., the Mental Competency Hearing before the Honorable Frank S. Szymanski - Wednesday, July 21, 1976.
2. Document: State of Michigan, Probate Court for the County of Wayne, in the Matter of Alexander Zolkewsky, Jr., Order Following hearing on Petition - Michigan, Dated July 21, 1976; Present, Honorable Frank S. Szymanski, Judge of Probate.
3. Document: State of Michigan, Probate Court for the County of Wayne, in the Matter of Alexander Zolkewsky, Jr., The Application for Admission by medical Certification and Petition for Admission and corresponding documents, Filed June 21, 1976.
4. Document: Wayne County General Hospital . . . Record Report, Alex Zolk, Jr., Dated June 24, 1976, Page #1.
5. Transcripts: State of Michigan, Probate Court for the County of Wayne, in the Matter of the Estate of: Alex Zolkewsky, Jr., the mental Competency Hearing before the Honorable Frank S. Szymanski - Judge, Wednesday, July 21, 1976.
6. Documents: Chief, Dearborn Heights Fire Department, my letter of request concerning the affirmed incident on the father and City of Dearborn Heights, City Clerk Office, record of Corporation Counsel.
7. Document: City of Dearborn Heights, Fire Chief, letter addressed to me.
8. Document: Wayne County General Hospital, Dated August 20, 1976, Alex Zolkewsky, Jr., Mental Examination.
9. Documents: Order of Examination and Transport, all three paragraphs, Ordered by Judge of Probate, Willis F. Ward, Dated June 21, 1976 and State of Michigan, Probate Court for the

County of Wayne, in the Matter of Alex Zolkewsky, Jr., the Order Following Preliminary Hearing - Michigan, Dated June 30, 1976 where present was Honorable Joseph J. Pernick, Judge of Probate.

10. Documents: Copy of Envelope from Michigan Department of State, Lansing P.B. Meter and First Class Postage, to Alex Robinson and Copy of Letter: Unable to Complete Request for Vehicle, noted box for Other reasons: Have only the last six years information and Department of State, Request for Record Information, Alex Robinson, Vehicle, Received March, 1986, Commercial Lookup, also Title Record, Registration Record.

11. Documents: Department of State Request for Record Information, Alex Robinson, Vehicle Received March, 1986, Commercial Lookup, also Title Record, Registration Record.

12. Documents: Marriage License, Wayne County, Michigan, between Alexander Zolkewsky, Sr., and Caroline C. Robinson, dated May 29, 1952 . . . and Certificate of Marriage, dated June 14, 1952, by a Pastor, in Hamtramck, Michigan . . . Immaculate Conception Ukrainian Catholic Church . . . and Wayne County General Hospital . . . Record Report, Alex Zolkewsky, Jr., dated June 24, 1976, Page #1, ending Page #4. Social Work Intern, Josephine Lampton, same document, Page #2 . . . Pertinent Social History.

13. Document: Letter dated April, 1972, The Senate, Lansing, Michigan, to Alex Zolkewsky, Jr., from State Senator David A. Plawecki.

14. Document: Michigan State University, Office of Financial Aids, to Alex Robinson, dated March, 1986.

15. Document: Typed up for me to place to the court, Michigan Department of Education, Scholarship Awards.

16. Documents: Ingham Medical Hospital, Lansing, Michigan, Employment Application, dated December 11, 1972, MSU Student Address, Position Orderly, on Alex Robinson and Education, MICHIGAN STATE UNIVERSITY, East Lansing, pre-medicine, also Work History, Employment, December, 1972. Voluntary Termination upon Request in February, 1974.

17. Document: Michigan State University, East Lansing,

Office of the Registrar, Official Record, Student Alex Robinson, From Fall 1972, Lyman Briggs School, until Spring 1975 when transferred to Wayne State University, Detroit, Michigan in Summer 1975.

18. Document: Wayne County General Hospital . . . Psychiatric Consultation, Dated June 21, 1976
. . . Examining Psychiatrist, "B. Ahn, M.D."

19. Document: Michigan State News, East Lansing, Michigan, Sports . . . Friday, June 4, 1976 . . . Spartans Look to Olympics . . . .

20. Document: Michigan State News, East Lansing, Michigan, Sports with Wednesday, June 30, 1976, also Lowe qualifies.

21. Documents: Personal Money Order, dated November 12, 1977, Pay to the Order of U.S. Olympic Committee, $50.00. Copy Not Negotiable. Alex Robinson and Personal Money Order, dated June 19, 1981, Pay to the Order of U.S. Olympic Society, Personal Check, dated September 11, 1985, Pay to the Order of U.S. Olympic Society, $19.88. Membership, Alex Robinson and United States Olympic Society, Alex Robinson, dated November, 1985, Bronze Laurel Member. Certificate.

22. Document: Lyman Briggs School, Michigan State University, Student Handbook.

23. Document: Department of State, Request for Record Information . . . Alex Robinson . . . Vehicle Information . . . 1973 Dodge B-100 Van . . . Title Record with Caroline Zolkewsky . . . June, 1973 to September, 1974.

24. Document: Savings Accounts . . . Certifies . . . 'Alex Robinson' . . . Beneficiary . . . Holds a Savings Deposit . . . "date July 1974 . . . Withdrawal of $1,000.00 with a remaining balance . . ."

25. Documents: Department of State, Request for Record Information . . . Alex Robinson . . . Vehicle Information: . . . 1968 Dodge Charger 2 Door . . . September 1975 to September 1976 and The Sunday Detroit News, September 5, 1976 . . . Section # Dodge . . . .

26. Document: Wayne County General Hospital . . . Record Report, Alex Zolkewsky, Jr., Dated June 24, 1976, Page #1,

same document - Page #5, Progress & Suspension Note, Dated August 30, 1976, same document - Page #6.

27. Document: Department of Health and Human Services, Social Security Administration, Report of Confidential Social Security Benefit Information, Alex Robinson, Beneficiary. Dated March 10, 1986.

CHAPTER 3

June 5, 1978

Summary

**Plaintiffs - Dearborn Heights Police Department individual officers,
Mrs. Caroline Zolkewsky, dictated to as a crippled mom, and her youngest son, Myron Zolkewsky.**

From the records, there are:
FOUR . . . Defendants simultaneously, this from legal initials and by Michigan Driver's License Identification, County of Wayne, State of Michigan.
This is affirmed by the plaintiffs.

Legal Initials and Identification	Estate of:
A. Z.	Dad
A. Z. J. R.	Sworn Family ID
A. Z. R. J.	But They Do Not Exist
A. R.	Eldest Son, Signed & Covered for Father.

Affirmations and documents were altered after June 14, 1978 and up to June 19, 1978, in the County of Wayne, State of Michigan. This took place in the presence of plaintiffs and other doctors, registered nurses, attendants, Detroit and Wayne County building employees of the Probate Court and its judges in the County of Wayne.

Data and items placed in files of one of the four, Alex Robinson, who was on an appeal process two years earlier, from 1976.

Affirmed five felony charges; affirmed five items of criminal misconduct:

One charge of larceny of mail, this with the United States Postal Service in Dearborn Heights.

One charge of larceny of money.

Two charges of vandalism:
      a.   Car motor of plaintiff.
      b.   Personal and real property of plaintiffs and interested parties and family.

One charge of Assault and Battery, Mother's Day, Sunday, May 14, 1978, supposedly on the mother. Treatment affirmed at Henry Ford Hospital - Fairlane, Dearborn, Michigan outpatient clinic.

*   *   *

I state that on June 5, 1978 an order of Examination and Transport[1] was upon my father, and that this document was altered on June 14, 1978, and further on in this case.[2] I will show and explain this later on in my behalf. The "arrest warrant from the judge" was altered by the individual officers in the Dearborn Heights Police Department, and the time period was June 14, 1978 up to June 19, 1978, as I figure. This was done, because I, Alex Robinson, was removed from my home at that time instead of my father, Alexander Zolkewsky, who was documented on the items discussed. The plaintiffs affirmed that Alexander Zolkewsky, my father, did commit those five felony charges, did commit the five charges of criminal misconduct, as permanent record in the County of Wayne, State of Michigan, to the judges involved. Essentially, I, Alex Robinson, did sign and cover for my dad in this matter, and yet all of these items occurring in 1978 and beyond are, of course, placed and filed in my permanent record in the County of Wayne, State of Michigan. Hence, I will show that I nor my father, whom I signed and covered for did commit the five felony charges, nor did either of us commit the five charges of criminal misconduct on the Court records.

I will also show that the plaintiffs, individual officers of Dearborn Heights Police Department, Caroline Zolkewsky, and Myron Zolkewsky, did commit PERJURY, CONTEMPT OF

COURT, and FRAUD upon the Judges, the Courts, the doctors, and several government-mandated offices that are involved in this case.

From the above documents on the court record, note that the main plaintiff is Caroline Zolkewsky, who is being dictated to as a crippled mom, and note her type and kind of printing and handwriting on these documents. Also, note on the white blank sheets attached to the documents and that are written in with plaintiffs data on this case. This printing and handwriting was done by a secondary plaintiff in the case.

Five numbered pages are attached to the documents of permanent record, originally blank sheets, filled in by the secondary plaintiff, Myron Zolkewsky, who also affirms the items along with the Dearborn Heights Police Department individual officers.[3,4] When the Dearborn Heights Police Department, with Caroline Zolkewsky, altered the documents from my father with his eldest son signing and covering for him, they also brought along the secondary plaintiff, Myron Zolkewsky, to also commit alterations of the court and permanent records. These were done after June 14, 1978.

Regarding the above attached sheets, the documents in this part of the case, note that all the numbered sentences are in the handwriting of Myron Zolkewsky, the secondary plaintiff. But also note the subject heading at the top of each numbered document: "Re: Alexander Robinson." These are printed by Myron Zolkewsky. Note this basic discrepancy, this error by the plaintiffs.

I state that these subject headings were inserted by the plaintiffs, especially Myron Zolkewsky, after June 14, 1978, after they have affirmed that Alexander Zolkewsky had committed the five charges of criminal misconduct, the five felony charges documented on this case. After I had signed and covered for my dad, on June 14, 1978, that is when the alterations took place by the plaintiffs in this case, for the permanent records in the County of Wayne, State of Michigan.

Hence:

(Same Documents - Page 1)

Sentence 3, . . . "he throws out mail and important

papers, ..."

(Same Documents - Page 1)

Sentence 9, ... "... in a ... (... a horizontal arrow, a horizontal vector,) then

(Same Documents - Page 2)

Continue sentence 9, ...(following a horizontal vector an equal sign ...) then comments.

What do comments, then a horizontal vector or horizontal arrow, then an equal sign, then finishing comments, mean as stated by the plaintiff? These items are in sentence number 9, and I would like the plaintiffs to further describe this data to the judges and the courts.

(Same Documents - Page 3)

Sentence 17, "does not hold a job."

This occurred by a Court Order, by most of the plaintiffs two years ago as stated to the judges at that time, and I was on appeal and just following orders of the court and judges.

Also note in the upper left corner, there is no comment of a continuation from previous pages, as the prior page has in its upper left corner.

Sentence 20, "He threatens to report us to ... Church Pastor ... He becomes very religious on Sunday only."

The plaintiffs state that having the behavior and habit of attending Sunday church services, without them, mind you, that this is a mental disease or mental illness along with the criminal misconduct items stated, of which I will claim that they are falsely documented statements by the plaintiffs in this case.

Sentence 23, "He has taken money in large amounts from family members."

(Same Documents - Page 4)

No comment of continuation in upper left corner of this page of attached sheets and documents from the plaintiffs.

Sentence 26, "On May 14, 1978 and June 4, 1978 he became violent."

Section (A): "He was confronted with evidence of destroying the youngest son's car motor on June 4, 1978 ... he deliberately damaged and destroyed the T.V. set, the china cabinet, the grandfather clock, plants, vases, etc. (A police report is at the Dearborn Hts. Station)."

Section (B): "On Mother's Day, May 14 . . . He would forcibly push the mother away by butting her with his head and right shoulder (much like a goat), he then took his right heel and jammed it on mother's right toes . . . (There is another police report). The mother had treatment at Fairlane Clinic, and was unable to wear a shoe due to swelling."

(Same Documents - Page 5)

There is no comment as to the continuation from previous pages in the upper left corner. Note sentence 33: "rarely leaves the house." I will prove this to be false.

I state that the plaintiffs, the Dearborn Heights Police Department individual officers, Caroline Zolkewsky, and secondary plaintiff Myron Zolkewsky, have committed PERJURY, CONTEMPT OF COURT, and FRAUD upon the Judges, the doctors, the Courts, and several government-mandated offices involved in this case. I will now prove my case on appeal with the following evidence.

"Magical Mystery Tour," <u>Album</u>, The Beatles.

Here the doctors and the hospital staff state for the record in Wayne County that Alexander Zolkewsky, my father, is also known as Alex Robinson, his eldest son, by legal initials, Michigan Driver's License identification, Social Security Identification, tax identification purposes in the Internal Revenue Service area and Treasury Department in Michigan, and by genetics and functions of mitosis and meiosis.[5,6]

I state that this document was altered from the original one, that is, with Alexander Zolkewsky, my father, on the record, to include his eldest son, Alex Robinson that this was altered by the doctors and hospital staff at the plaintiff's request, at that time period of June 14, 1978 and beyond. These items occurred when I signed and covered for my father's five felony charges and five criminal acts of misconduct that were on record at the time of June 14, 1978, in the County of Wayne.

Next I will show that I was involved in the County of Wayne Vocational Rehabilitation Program, by a court order from July,

1976. This came from the judges as a result of my non-employment and disability status within the area of Dearborn Heights.

I will prove that the plaintiffs refused to comply with the judges and court's order for me, Alex Robinson, to be involved in this Vocational Rehabilitation program.

I was forced to withdraw on June 5, 1978, when I was transported to the Wayne County Psychiatric Hospital upon the "arrest warrant" or Court Order to Transport of Alexander Zolkewsky, my father.[7]

This was during final examinations in Spring 1978, and I telephoned the Wayne State University Student Ombudsman, the professors of my courses in my vocational rehabilitation program at WSU, and the Wayne State University Student Legal Aid. They received my information over the phone, and encouraged me to salvage with incompletes the Spring term of 1978 for later final grades. But all three areas did not agree and I, Alex Robinson, the eldest son of Alexander Zolkewsky, the father, and head of household, was placed in the mental hospital for dad, even according to the documents presented to the doctors on June 5, 1978. The Ombudsman stated that he would help me to obtain the incompletes, but that I should go to trial for my father anyhow. The professors advised me to seek legal counsel and to obtain my father's written permission, forwarded to the doctors, in order to have an appointment with his son and the doctors. The Wayne State University Student Legal Aid attorneys stated that I was talking about family law, and I was stating a mathematical probability of zero, but they said to have my court-appointed counsel contact them at WSU so that I could receive the incomplete grades, even with no money refunded!

I eventually made up the incomplete grades and transferred elsewhere in Wayne County. Also, I had to leave the Detroit Department of Transportation Bus Line of Crosstown Route on Warren Avenue, so as not to be removed from it again in Dearborn Heights as had happened to me on June 5, 1978, in the evening coming from the WSU campus. I was removed from the bus route for my father according to the records on June 5, 1978.

*   *   *

I'm not sure of the date, but Dearborn Heights Police Department Officers arrived at the Ford Motor Company, Rouge Steel Plant, Dearborn, located at Michigan Avenue and Miller Road. They removed my dad from his employment with security and proceeded west on Michigan Avenue. They went to the proper offices at the Wayne County Psychiatric Hospital. With doctors and hospital staff, they asked my father, who was still punched in as an hourly worker back up the road in Dearborn, to place his signature on the court documents that are in the files of my own case from two years prior, 1976. My father just did what was necessary to expedite the matter of Alex Robinson, his son, sitting upstairs for him. The officers then returned my father to work.[8]

In 1979, the year earlier, I had been taken from the Crosstown bus lines in Dearborn Heights from the WSU campus, this for my father, Alexander Zolkewsky, affirmed by the plaintiff on the court records but in the eldest son's files in the County of Wayne. My dad could have lost his Ford Motor pension if I did not sign and cover for him at the time in June, 1978.

By signing and covering for dad, he did not receive penalties from the Internal Revenue Service nor did he lose his insurance and control of his family business with his son.

"Taxman," <u>Revolver</u>, The Beatles.

I state that there is a false date stamped upon this other Order in the records, where the date should have been after June 14, 1978 and not as stamped as June 7, 1978. The first Order of Examination and Transport does not have any stamped nor filing date placed upon it, that was presented earlier in the above discussion.

Also this document, another Order, has filed upon it: "A True Copy . . . Deputy Probate Register with signature upon it." The first Order of Examination and Transport presented earlier does not have such verification, but is placed as the main document earlier in the sequence of these documents compared to this other document presented.

Also, in the matter of Alexander Zolkewsky, my father, this was changed with a comma and the letters added of "Jr." This was done by the plaintiffs upon the doctors and hospital staff, and to be placed in the records of me, the defendant, Alex Robinson, instead of the records of my father, Alexander Zolkewsky. This alteration of the physician's certificate took place after June 14, 1978 and involved the plaintiffs. Note that the entire subject of this matter, a Mr. Alexander Zolkewsky, Jr., was not documented at one time on the one hospital staff typewriter. But two separate times and two separate typewriters were involved in placing the document of my father and then another person, my old name which was not to be used at this time for identification, that both of these ended up after alteration took place on these court records.

Note the small letter "r" in Alexander, and also note very closely the small letter "r" in the junior abbreviation. By looking very closely, it is obvious that the horizontal line of the small letter "r" in "Jr" is completely different from the horizontal line of the small letter "r" in "Alexander." I state that this was not done at the exact time, and the alterations of my father on the Physicians Certificate took place after June 14, 1978, by someone else on an entirely different typewriter than the one used by the doctor's hospital staff initially. I state that these alterations took place accordingly from the plaintiffs actions. My father was directly involved in this situation, but I, his eldest son, did take his place by force, in order to resolve this matter from the plaintiffs and the individual police officers, in this case.

The doctor personally examined, by legal initials, A. Z.--Alexander Zolkewsky--as stated and affirmed by the plaintiffs on the permanent records starting on June 5, 1978. The documents appearing to the doctor on June 6, 1978 correlate and match the doctor's observations of my father, as testified by the petition from the plaintiffs. As you well know, I, Alex Robinson, the eldest son, was in front of the doctors on June 6, 1978 for the session of Alexander Zolkewsky, my dad, according to the documents on the case. I was removed from the Vocational Rehabilitation program at Wayne State University in order to appear for him at this time.

About June 9, 1978, my court-appointed attorney, Mr. Craig, approached me and asked me why all my wallet identification as to who I was, that is, just my empty wallet, was in my personal belongings with the hospital staff only, and I had no personal documents. The doctors and hospital staff stated to the attorney that the defendant's data was agreed upon by the doctors, the plaintiffs, and the individual police officers of Dearborn Heights Police Department to be falsified documents, false identification, and false papers. This was relayed to me by my court-appointed lawyer.

I stated to Mr. Craig that I was Alex Robinson, not my father as recorded on the court documents in front of him, and that I was removed from the VocRehab program at the Wayne State University Business studies field and even my final examinations. As we prepared for my dad's trial in about a week, I kept saying that I was not the person documented on his records, that the person was my father. Furthermore, the five felony charges, the five alleged criminal misconduct items were not done either by my dad nor myself. I will prove this in awhile. My court-appointed attorney stated that in family law, I was discussing impossibility, and he did not want to further discuss the matter.

So, I angrily wrote down my name with my WSU student identification, my Social Security Number, and my driver's license. I gave him about a dollar in my coin change and asked my attorney to call WSU Legal Aid for Students and the Ombudsman. I also handed him my penciled paper defense statement, stating that I was taken by records instead of the father, recorded as Alexander Zolkewsky on the affirmed item noted.

On the morning of June 14, 1978, Mr. Craig returned to me and quietly stated to me that I was telling the exact truth of the matter, and furthermore, he believed that I was innocent of being a maniac or a psychotic. We then discussed our strategy for the proper moves to have me released for my father.

We agreed that since my identification documents, licenses, and student I.D. were thrown in the garbage by the hospital staff and doctors because of the suggestions of the Dearborn Heights

Police Department individual officers, I could not be in trial for my father. Then we could prove this event as it stands to the courts. That is, that I, Alex Robinson, was on trial for the father as recorded by the plaintiffs Alexander Zolkewsky for the five felony charges and the five criminal acts of misconduct affirmed by the plaintiffs. I would prove that Alex Robinson did not do the above items on the documents and also that my father Alexander Zolkewsky as court ordered, that he did not do those acts either. We did not have any valid I.D. at the time to have me released to my incompletes and to bring my father in to the judges and the courts.

So as my attorney discussed with the hospital staff and doctors with his long oration of his client's situation pertaining to them, actually time allowed for me, Alex Robinson, on June 14, 1978 to sign and cover for Alexander Zolkewsky, my father, by placing the signature of Alex Robinson upon permanent court documents of Alexander Zolkewsky that were presented earlier. I have also showed that from the afternoon of June 14, 1978, up until June 19, 1978, all the alterations made by the plaintiffs, the doctors, and the hospital staff and court staff to the court documents were done under direct orders of the plaintiffs and individual officers of the Dearborn Heights Police Department.

Also note on this above document that the capital letter "R" in Alexander and the capital letter "R" in Robinson are different. Notice the noun Alexander--the "R" has the line at the 45 degree angle from the circle of the letter, which ends in a curvature. Note the "R" in Robinson: it has the line at the 45 degree angle from the circle of the letter, which ends in a serif.

From June 14, 1978 up until June 21, 1978, I was incarcerated in the mental hospital for my father as the eldest son, where the trial was dismissed and I was not. After the three days I spoke to the doctors and the staff, and they stated that I was not who I was purported to be according to their data from the plaintiffs, and that my outpatient psychiatrist, whom I had been checking in with every month or so over the last two years, was not able to be reached for my positive identification for the time being. I started to check his outpatient office from 9 to 5 during the week, and he knew about my program at Wayne State

University and did not know about my father involved in the court records at this time. I could not reach him by pay telephone.

I state that neither my father nor myself committed the five felony charges psychopathia, that we both did not do the five criminal acts of misconduct as affirmed by the plaintiffs in the case.

My discharge documents were also altered.[9] They now read another individual, a fifth individual for this part of the case, whose legal initials are A. J. Z, Alexander Jr. Zolkewsky. This was altered from the original, which carried my father's name.

Again, note that the noun Alexander and next to it the abbreviation Jr. Notice the small letter "r" in the noun Alexander, and notice the small letter "r" in the noun Jr. If you look very, very closely, one will note the vast difference in the two letters.

Also note that on my birth certificate, my old name was, legal initials, A. Z. Jr., or Alexander Zolkewsky Junior. It is not A. J. Z., or Alex Junior Zolkewsky. This alteration was done between June 14, 1978 and July 3, 1978 on my records of the case.

Note the comments made regarding my discharge:

Reason for Admission: Patient was admitted with a petition . . . Provisional Diagnosis Mental Status on Admission: Patient was superficially cooperative, clean and neat, quiet and defensive in revealing himself. He was tense and very guarded. He is oriented x3. Affect is extremely cautious. He is over-productive. Psychiatric therapy: Although patient was admitted involuntarily. Mental Status on Discharge: He was quiet, pleasant, seemed to be comfortable, calm, and he was cooperative. He appeared to be motivated for his aftercare follow-up and he is to see Dr. Uddyback in 2-4 days. Prognosis: Fair. Final Diagnosis: Remained the same. Signed Teresita Timban, M.D., Rec'd. 6-21-78/Trans. 7-3-78.

I also state that it took the doctors 14 days to finish documenting and transcribing my records. This is wrong and very unusual, and is based upon the altering of all permanent documents involved in this part of the case, where my father, Alexander Zolkewsky appeared on all the documents, and I, his eldest son, did sign and cover for him.

* * *

My Application for Admission on June 5, 1978 accuses me of the following: "He throws out mail and important papers," and "He has taken money in large amounts from family members." I did not steal any mail from the plaintiffs. They do not have any verifiable proof of that. Furthermore, I did not steal any of the plaintiffs' paychecks from the mail, nor my father's checks from the business, and then falsely endorse them for the money. I state further that the plaintiffs do not have any of their bank data, that is, the photocopies or the canceled checks. There is no way to show that these checks were falsely endorsed. I state there is no evidence to support larceny of mail, and there is no evidence to support larceny of money from the mail or otherwise.

"[On June 4, 1978 he became violent. He was confronted with evidence of destroying the youngest son's car motor on June 4, 1978 . . . (A police report is at the Dearborn Hts. Station).]"

I state that the plaintiffs cannot show or produce evidence that I made vandalism upon a car motor or anyone living at our home. There are no insurance reports to show the basis of this charge, no mechanics reports, bills, or estimates showing a complete rebuilding of a car motor or a car engine once destroyed. There is no insurance documentation and police verification with towing to an engine-rebuilding mechanic's establishment, where the new engine or a new rebuilt engine could have been placed in any of the plaintiff's vehicles with insurance coverage as well. No such data ever existed, nor does it exist at present.

Also, I did not vandalize anybody's personal property at my father's house, since I state that there is not any evidence presented such as insurance reports, pictures, estimates for replacement of articles, or payments from homeowner's insurance policies. I state that this data does not exist, nor did that data ever exist before.

Their lies continue: "On Mother's Day, May 14 . . . he would forcibly push the mother away by butting her with his head and right shoulder (much like a goat), he then took his right heel and jammed it on mother's right toes . . . (There is another police report). The mother had treatment at Fairlane Clinic, and was unable to wear a shoe due to swelling."

Note the medical reports from my mother's injury:[10,11]

Brought to ER by: Son . . . Current Medications . . . Yes . . . Diuretics, slow potassium. Date of Injury 5-14-78 . . . Complaint . . . Injured Rt. Foot . . . Blood Pressure 170/106 . . . History/Physical/Treatment . . . Pt.s. son stepped on her toes today, increased pain and Pt. known hypertensive and history of bowel surgery . . . (bypass?) 10 years ago . . . Examination . . . Obesity . . . Pedal Edema . . . Right 4th toe swollen and tender to touch . . . Diagnosis (Final): Blunt Trauma right 4th toe . . . X-Ray right 4th toe . . . Nurse's Signature . . . Disposition: Elevate foot . . . extra diuretic tonight . . . Acetyl Salicylic Acid A.S.A. or aspirin.

also:

History: . . . on toes.[12] Now complains of numbness . . . Referring Physician Service . . . E.R. . . . Examination Requested . . . Bone: Toes . . . Right . . . Zolkewsky . . . Right Toes 5/14/78: A fracture is not identified . . . Physician's Signature.

As a pre-medicine student with a minor in that field and ambulance medic training, I state the following conclusions for the data involved in this case:

#1. From the data above, there is no indication that the above resulting items occurred from an assault and battery supposedly on the mother as a plaintiff in this case.

#2. From the data above, these data items all combine together to form the basis of what is really occurring at this time, before this time period, and even today years after this time period.

Current medications are diuretics, slow potassium. Her blood pressure is 170/106, which shows very high and very abnormal systolic and diastolic measurements of this woman's heart functions, rates, and motions at all times. This is an extreme range, which causes the metabolism problems seen here. Increased pain, this would occur with the above conditions. Patient is known to be hypertensive, and this can be verified for at least the last ten years. The patient has a history of bowel surgery, this due to improper eating rates and habits for at least ten years from 1978. Obesity means increased body weight, increased water retention, increased fat retention, improper dieting, and improper digestion of nutrients. This causes a bloating or swelling effect on this person in all areas, limbs, skin, facial tissues, and extremities including the legs. The examination noted pedal edema, or severe swelling of the legs and the feet, including the toes of the feet. Hence from the above, the right 4th toe is swollen and tender to touch.

#3. But if this were the result of an assault and battery, all the toes and the front of the foot would have been severely damaged as testified and affirmed by the plaintiffs, and not just a singular toe with slight swelling, which the data above states. Even tight and uncomfortable shoes on swollen legs and swollen feet could cause this. Hence, the final diagnosis: "blunt trauma right 4th toe, with the disposition of elevating foot, extra diuretic tonight, take aspirin to reduce swelling as an end result." All of these are directly a result of Caroline Zolkewsky's conditions, and not from a supposed assault and battery by the defendant, as affirmed by the plaintiffs.

#4. Also, Caroline Zolkewsky states she complains of numbness in the toes. I state this is due to her problems listed above. Also, there were no fractures in any bones of the right toes. The affirmations of the plaintiffs are lies, and this assault and battery never occurred, except maybe with someone else, or in the plaintiffs' malfunctioning heads.

To continue on, I show a report made by my mother's doctor:[13] "Weight 233 1/4 lbs. . . . gaining weight . . . swelling left leg . . . taking blood pressure pills . . . blood pressure 150/90 . . . #4 Obesity." A test later that year showed similar results, along with several other tests up to the date of the supposed assault and battery and beyond.[14]

Conclusively, all the facts and data show that there is no basis of an assault and battery upon the mother, Caroline Zolkewsky. I, Alex Robinson, did not commit this mythical act. There is no evidence to support the affirmations of all the plaintiffs in this entire case, and in fact, all the evidence I have presented shows clearly that what is affirmed by the plaintiffs is not true at all. The facts presented in the last few paragraphs show clearly that the woman's problem is very severe in human functions, and not caused by the defendant in this case.

ENDNOTES CHAPTER 3

1. Document: Order of Examination and Transport, all three paragraphs, ordered by the Judge of Probate, Ira G. Kaufman, dated June 5, 1978, in the Matter of A. Z. or Alexander Zolkewsky and in the Matter of A. Z. R., Jr. or Alexander Zolkewsky Robinson, Jr. and in the Matter of A. R. or Alex Robinson by attachment to File No. in the County of Wayne.

2. Documents: State of Michigan, Probate Court for the County of Wayne, in the Matter of Alexander Zolkewsky, in the matter of A. Z., Jr. or Alexander Zolkewsky, Jr. Robinson or in the Matter of A. Z. Jr. or Alexander Zolkewsky Robinson, Jr. or in the Matter of A. R. or Alex Robinson by the File No. in County of Wayne. The Application for Admission by Medical Certification and Petition for Admission and corresponding documents, filed June 5, 1978.

3. Document: Letter from Walter P. Reuther Psychiatric Hospital, State of Michigan, to Alex Robinson, Metropolitan Regional Psychiatric Hospital from June 5, 1978 to June 21, 1978. "While a patient . . . your name on our records was Alex Zolkewsky, Jr., also known as Alex Robinson."

4. Documents: Psychiatric Record Copy, items outlined in ink. State of Michigan, Probate Court for the County of Wayne, in the Matter of A. Z., Alex Zolkewsky. In the Matter of A. Z. Jr., Alexander Zolkewsky, Jr. Robinson, or in the Matter of A. Z. R. Jr., Alexander Zolkewsky Robinson, Jr., or in the Matter of A. R., Alex Robinson, attached to File No. in the County of Wayne. Application for Admission by Medical Certification and Petition for Admission and corresponding documents, Filed on June 5, 1978, Paragraph #2 . . . ". . . See attached sheets . . .", Paragraph #3 . . . Admission by petition only:, Paragraph #5 . . . Paragraph #6 . . ., Paragraph #7 . . ., Paragraph #9 . . . Prayer . . . Declaration . . . penalty of perjury . . . dated "June 5," 19"78" . . .

signed Caroline Zolkewsky. Also, Paragraph #2 . . . ". . . See attached sheets . . ."

5. Document: Psychiatric Record Copy, items outlined in ink. Michigan Department of Mental health, Formal Voluntary Admission Application, to the Director of Metropolitan Regional Psychiatric Hospital, signed by Odie Uddyback, M.D., dated 6-14-78. "The formal voluntary admission of Alexander Zolkewsky, A.K.A. Robinson."

6. Documents: Marriage License, Wayne County, Michigan, between Alexander Zolkewsky and Caroline Robinson, dated May 29, 1952 . . . and Certificate of Marriage, dated June 14, 1952 by a Pastor, in Hamtramck, Michigan, Immaculate Conception Ukrainian Catholic Church.

7. Document: Wayne State University Academic Record, Detroit, Michigan, Admitted 9/75, Alex Robinson, Sophomore transferred from MSU. "Winter Quarter 1977" Same document - Page 2, "Transfer to Pre-Bus. Adm., . . . Winter Quarter 1978 . . . Curr: Finance, Full Credit . . . Spring Quarter 1978 . . . all 12 credit hours . . . Incomplete Grades . . . Summer Quarter 1978 . . . Complete Withdrawal."

8. Document: Evidence from Ford Motor Company. Alexander Zolkewsky, Steel Division management announcement. June 1979 Official Retirement with Pension Rights.

9. Document: Metropolitan Regional Psychiatric Hospital. Name, legal initials A. J. Z., Alexander Jr. Zolkewsky. Discharge Summary. Date of Admission: 6-5-78. Date of Discharge: 6-21-78. Teresita Timban, M.D. Rec'd. 6-21-78/trans. 7-3-78.

10. Document: Henry Ford Hospital, Fairlane Center, Dearborn, Michigan . . . sent to Mr. Alexander Zolkewsky . . . Regarding: Caroline Zolkewsky . . . Emergency Memo and X-Ray Reports on 5-14-78.

11. Document: Henry Ford Hospital, Fairlane Center, Emergency Care, dated 5-14-78, Name, Zolkewsky, Caroline.

12. Document: Fairlane Center, Radiology Department, Request and Report, dated May 14, 1978 Zolkewsky, Caroline.

13. Document: George Kadian, M.D., Endocrinology and

Metabolism . . . Patient: Caroline Zolkewsky. Date of test: 2-5-75.

14. Document: Caroline Zolkewsky . . . dated Oct. 17, '75. "Weight 236 . . . dizzy spells . . . blood pressure 160/90."

CHAPTER 4

Now I present a piece of evidence, retrieved from a garbage can in my father's house. It is a bank record:[1] "August 1974, Balance $6,000.00. Then, August 1977, withdrawals for the beneficiary's university studies as a freshman. Note on May 30, 1978: withdrawals of $1,600.00 for the Commodities Markets Exchanges for Corn Futures, as written by the Trustee, Caroline Zolkewsky. Zero balance as the result at this date. Canceled."

I state that the plaintiff and the secondary plaintiff, Caroline and Myron Zolkewsky, used college trust fund money to speculate on the commodities markets, just one item, without proper research nor proper brokers applications of speculating. They did this without my father's knowledge, nor my own. With their one item, Corn Futures, they did not diversify on the commodities markets with options, indexes, and shares in combination with their $1,600.00 gamble. They lost, with no insurance, and just like the professional brokers and dealers and speculators might lose, and then they probably realized the severe problems they had as a team. They probably did receive from the volatile markets, not protected, 1% from $1,600.00, or just $16.00. I assume this occurred from their behavior just six calendar days later when my father, Alexander Zolkewsky, appeared on the judge's Order of Examination and Transport to the mental hospital, on June 5, 1978.

They were behaving strangely in those days. Myron Zolkewsky was a Criminal Justice major at his university, and therefore had his Dearborn Heights Police Department references and connections. He was involved with his mother in removing my dad from his estate, his employment, his pension rights, his income tax service, his head of household rights, his constitutional rights in America and in Michigan, and my father's Sunday religious services as well.

Well, somehow I, Alex Robinson, his eldest son, was removed from the Crosstown Bus Route from the Detroit bus service on the Detroit and Dearborn Heights borderline off of West Warren Avenue, coming from Wayne State University, of which transcripts were presented earlier. It seems that the individual officers needed to prevent me from appealing my case from the prior two years, and all six of them ordered me to be placed in the mental hospital on the night of June 5, 1978.

This is the best explanation I can produce from the evidence that I have brought forward to the appellate courts. I feel that the plaintiffs should show any and all of their evidence, and further to state their explanations as to the basics of the case.

I present the next items for I was involved in my appellate processes of the case:[2,3] "Victim's Name: Alex Robinson, Person Reporting Crime. No. of Offenders: Unknown. Vehicle: '72 Mercury 2 Door, Black/Blue. Victim is principal driver of vehicle registered to complainant . . .. This a.m. found left lower section of windshield had been smashed in, large concrete section on street, vehicle also struck by car, causing damage to left front fender . . . refer to other complaint number."

"Accident date: 8-30-80. On Dale . . . Vehicle: Black/Blue. Year: '72. Away-owner: Alexander Zolkewsky, 8090 Dale, Dearborn Hts. Accident description and remarks: Refer to Other Dept. Report Complaint No. . . . No paint left on vehicle. The other vehicle could have either backed into this vehicle or could have struck vehicle while moving forward. See Diagram. Also Insurance Co: AAA Agency . . . Struck Vehicle: Principal complainant's son, Alex Robinson, same address as owner. Vehicle struck between 1:30 a.m. & 9:30 a.m. on 8/30/80."

First of all, note the intra-departmental coding on the above document just referred to. I am referring to "Hit & Run . . ." in the upper left hand corner, and then in the upper right hand corner of the same document. I state this occurred because I was involved in my appellate court processes at Madonna College in Livonia, Michigan, in the paramedic training program.

I assume that I was not going to be permitted in the County of Wayne to proceed in my bachelor's degree program as an Emergency Medical Technician at the college. Luckily, my dad's insurance coverage repaired the damages to our car, and I continued.

Next I show:[4]

"Myron Zolkewsky. Admission by petition only. I therefore pray that the subject of this petition be admitted by order of said court to a suitable hospital or facility. I declare the contents thereof are true to the best of my knowledge. Dated 11-25-80. Signed, Myron Zolkewsky."

In summary, in November, 1980, there were the affirmations of the case records of several individuals, including the defendant, Alex Robinson. The affirmations were continued individually by the primary plaintiff, Myron Zolkewsky, whereby full agreement and swearing of truth pertaining to entire case history of defendant, Alex Robinson and affirmed felony charges, all 11 of them, all 11 criminal acts of misconduct charges as documented upon the defendant, and even others.[5]

Next, I present these documents involved in my case history records:[6]

"8090 Dale St. . . . Victim's Name . . . Complainant . . . Nature of Injuries . . . Nose and body had marks and slight swelling . . . No. of Offenders: 4. Vehicle: '75 or '76 Monarch or Granada. Color: Dark. Narrative: Complainant states that above defendants were in above vehicle and complainant came home in his vehicle . . . The defendant's vehicle was blocking complainant's driveway. Complainant blew horn at them, when their vehicle bumped his . . . All four defendants exited vehicle and began harassing complainant . . . When complainant stated he would call police . . . defendant #1 punched complainant in face. This followed by defendants #1, 2, and 3 punching and kicking complainant."

Also:[7]

Nature of injuries: 12-18-80 . . . red marks and slight swelling to nose and body . . . he had a broken nose per X-Ray and he had contusions . . . he was kicked in the left side of head . . . he possibly has a fractured upper jaw . . . .

4-15-81 Detective Lieutenant asked complainant to describe his injuries again. Complainant stated he had contusions on his face, where he was kicked in his temple. His nose was fractured, but did not require re-setting. He stated he was also kicked in his right elbow, right inner knee, and right inner thigh . . . He was punched repeatedly by all three; one in front and two off to the side. Complainant stated he thought they were going to try to kill him. Complainant stated he never got knocked down - he managed to stay on his feet . . . Reporting Officer . . . Detective Lieutenant . . . Records.

Next I show:[8]
"Treatment . . . Emergency Room . . . #1 Contusions Left Face . . . #2 Fracture Volmer or nose
. . . Illness began: Attacked yesterday . . . Injury Occurred: . . . Right Nostril breathing problem . . . Disposition . . . Instruction Sheets: Contusion, Ice to Left Face and Skull and Nose, and to see Plastic Surgery."
And:[9,10]
"Gang Assault and Battery Investigation . . . False lead . . . 1-3-81 . . . Detective Lieutenant phoned complainant to state his lead did not pan out."
Next I show these documents:[11]
"Notice that all the important data for this case, all of it has been removed for security reasons for the defendants, that these items are outlined in ink."
I kept the get-away vehicle's Michigan license plate identification to myself since the night in question, when it ran the stop sign at our end of the street in the lighted area near my house. I held it until the third Sunday in January, Super Bowl Sunday 1981, then stated that precious information to what I believed was a neutral group within the Dearborn Heights Police Department, and not to any individual police officers nor detectives who were plaintiffs in my court cases from four years before with the other plaintiffs and their criminal justice friend in my dad's house at the time. For I felt and still feel that this gang assault and battery was wholly connected, tied in with my appellate processes at

Madonna College in Livonia in my Paramedic training on the bachelor's degree level, which I will show in transcripts in awhile.

I was barely able to see on that night, but was lucky enough to catch the car escaping with the gang as it went through the stop sign in the brightly lit area on Ann Arbor Trail and Dale St. I had tremendously blurred vision, but caught the license plates just in time, and I just kept it to myself until I felt a more proper time for adding this data to my basic reports.

But from the above paragraphs of data items, and further on, it seems that the defendants are connected with my entire case record in the County of Wayne, and have a basis through the individual police officers and their references who are the plaintiffs on this case along with the other plaintiffs at my house and even the "C.J. buddy," Myron Zolkewsky, presented earlier as a primary plaintiff.

Finally these documents:[12]

"Date of Crime: 12-18-80 . . . Gang Assault and Battery . . . Place . . . Hines Park area and 8090 Dale . . . Complaint No. . . . Noted Important . . . Investigation No and Yes both marked . . . Disposition of Case . . . Case Closed . . . Insufficient Evidence . . . dated 4-8-82."

I state that the above documents in files in the Dearborn Heights Police Department, from me being able to report the above paragraphs and the forms, are directly related to my case in the Courts of Wayne County, State of Michigan. I state that the above offenders are related somehow with the individual police officers as plaintiffs of Dearborn Heights Police Department with the other plaintiffs in my case as a defendant.

I also state that the offenders are either friends, family connections, work references, college and/or high school friends, either drinking buddies and/or contacts of the plaintiffs on my court case. Whether they are references from contacts of Myron Zolkewsky, the Misses, or the individual police officers from the 1978 or 1976 episodes remains to be seen.

I refer back to documents just presented, which are:[13]

Note the areas, "#37 Name of Detective . . . Notified and Time . . . a.m. or p.m. . . . where this area is left as blank space . . . instead in #11 Social Security Number is the time noted in units . . . and #16 Location of Incident and Addition . . . Detective Lieutenant notified in police case."

From the above data presented, I state that this is intra-departmental coding in order to resolve my case without any incident or to complete what I assume was the order from the judges in the County of Wayne, and that was to not let me finish training at Madonna College in a management capacity or even in a trainee position. I will show items in awhile pertaining to this.

"Two of Us," <u>Let It Be</u>, The Beatles.

Next I present:[14]
Inventory . . . Personal Property . . . Estate's Interest . . . Zero . . . Guardian did not receive any Social Security payments . . .' This notation by plaintiff Attorney Anatol Zolkewsky for Guardian Caroline Zolkewsky whereas neither of them were ordered or applied by their I.D. to receive Social Security payments . . .' . . . Ward has receipt of Social Security payments . . . Estate's Interest . . . Zero . . .' . . . Documented that the ward or defendant did receive sums of benefits greater than zero, from the Social Security Administration by Court Order and placed in Wayne County files . . . This opposite situation of realistic data was stated by plaintiff . . . Anatol Zolkewsky . . .' . . . Signature . . . Caroline Zolkewsky.

And I present:[15]

Guardian, Final Account to Sept. 14, 1981. Receipts . . . Note: Guardian did not have the receipt of Social Security payments . . . This item noted by plaintiff Anatol Zolkewsky but as discussed earlier, neither of them were ordered or applied by I.D. for Social Security payments to either of them; receipts . . . the receipt of Social Security payments . . . Total $ . . . (Blank space) . . . This item noted by the plaintiff Anatol Zolkewsky but is wrong because there was receipt of sums of benefits, not zero, that were accounted for on case records of Social Security Administration, and the Courts . . . I wish to resign as Guardian.

"Hearing November 2, 1981, . . . Petition to Terminate Guardian before Judge Anthony J. Szymanski, Judge of Probate . . . on date . . . Discharged Guardian and Bond Terminated . . . this for estate of legal initials . . . A. R. Z. . . . Alexander Robinson Zolkewsky as documented for Wayne County Probate

Court records, State of Michigan."

Further along:

Madonna College, Livonia, Michigan, Certificate of Achievement. Degree, Bachelor of Science, dated 7-26-1982. Major: Bank or Financial Services Administration. Alex Robinson, associated with minors in: Basic Emergency Medical Services and also with the minor in pre-medicine studies. Admitted 10-29-79 with Advanced Standing. Wayne State University transfer and also Michigan State University transfer. Degree Major Grade Point Average: 3.00 and Cumulative Grade Point Average: 2.90.

"Lady Madonna," Hey Jude, The Beatles.

I was told by the Director of EMT, a lady Ph.D. and Registered Nurse, along with other paramedical professors at Madonna College, that I was not allowed to continue, and I was incompetent to be in the Bachelor's program as a paramedical anywhere in the State of Michigan. Furthermore, I was to leave the college at once.

By the way, I paid them for the above items . . .

So I transferred to the Business and Computer Division and was accepted into the Banking or Financial Services Administration major curriculum area by those professors. Hence, this semester, Winter 1980 shown above, I also started my Bachelor's program in an acceptable major according to Madonna College Academic Committees.

Then notice:

Winter 1981 semester GPA: about 3.00, and the Cumulative GPA: 3.063, and the coding T.H.P.

Further on:

The next semester, Summer 1981. Semester GPA: 3.00, but the Cumulative GPA is 2.788 with the coding M.T.H.P., and this nowhere else on the entire transcript. That is, this specific coding is not to be found in any other area.

I assume this was because of my court orders from the last decade in the County of Wayne, State of Michigan since July, 1976.

But I also was in the process of my appeal from July, 1976 with affirmed attorneys.

Hence, notice:

Summer 1982. This was the final semester where upon I finished my Bachelor's program for a college degree, a job skill, with my two minors and major.

In late July, 1982, the two primary plaintiffs and the one secondary plaintiff called the Dearborn Heights Police Department to my dad's house and stated that I was not allowed to have this completed. They proceeded to falsely state more felony charges psychosis, falsely state psychopathia and falsely state more criminal acts of misconduct upon me. These individual police officers talked with the plaintiffs and then left, and later on I left for the evening.

I was encouraged by my professors to take the Graduate Management Admission Test, even with my disability and the appellate court processes of my case in the County of Wayne. I scored a 380, which is equivalent to a good C grade.

I then noticed an ad in the paper, which stated that the Navy had business/financial management positions. I conferred at the time with the pastor from my church in Dearborn Heights, who was a U.S. Navy Reserve Chaplain in this area, about starting the application processes. He encouraged me to go ahead. I took examinations and wrote other documents at the U.S. Naval Armory in Detroit. This was during March of 1983.

I was telephoned by officers there and told to come in for a consultation. While there, I was told I would not be able to become a U.S. Navy Officer, here, there, or anywhere. Then I was asked to leave the naval armory.

You see, I was desperate for employment and could not find any work in the private sector or even the government of the public sector, and tried my best in this area.

My pastor told me that I had severe problems with all the above because of the last seven years of lies placed on my record. The above even affected me in the process of enlistment in the U.S. Navy trainee program, for starting a career which was completely curtailed and stopped from July, 1976. I felt that I would not be able to even begin a work or work ethic record of employment with my disability status in the USA.

But I continued on.

In April, I went and applied for basic entry into the U.S. Army. It took me a week to bring in the documents and to take the entrance exams in Livonia, at a base located on I-96 near Levan Road, near my alma mater, Madonna College. In late April, I discussed this with the pastor of my church in Dearborn Heights. He said to bring the records of incompetence and insanity to the attention of the Army sergeants immediately, if not sooner, for he did not know that I was doing this action on our behalf. This was the first time I went to downtown Detroit, to the County of Wayne, Probate Court Files and Records Department to even look at what was there upon me. I did not have the $100.00 for all the records, so with about $20.00 I took whatever I could, and went directly to the Army sergeants in Livonia.

After the sergeants were in conference for about an hour, I realized their anger towards me and anger upon me for not presenting these documents sooner. They stated I had to end the application process immediately, and not proceed further, especially not continue into OCS or they would shoot me on sight. I was ordered to leave the Army offices. Good thing that I showed all the information that they had from the authorities in the County of Wayne, State of Michigan, which they stated helped to determine my non-eligibility for any career because of my status. Further, upon leaving, I was handed a document called, "The High Cost of Dropping Out."

Upon leaving the Army Military Counselor in Livonia, Michigan, I went to my pastor in Dearborn Heights. He explained to me that it was best that I begin an appellate court process to prove, if I could, that the documents and their contents were not true, and then to get started with a career. I replied that I had no funds, no income from disability or otherwise, and a victim-plaintiff father who was not helpful in his marriage towards anyone.

So, we figured that I should seek any basic employment offered in the public sector and maybe the private sector in the Detroit and Wayne County area, and I continued.

I was court-ordered in July, 1976, not to be able to work or seek employment as a bartender and bar manager because of the orders of the judges and the prosecution. This was all based on affirmations of the plaintiffs and the Dearborn Heights Police Department from the past to the time of 1976 and even into the future from July, 1976, and even to the present time in 1986. I realized I had been involved in something serious and life threatening, in regards to career and citizenship.

Because I had the records of insanity and incompetence, I must show the items that are upcoming, and the resulting incidents that occurred from this.

It was over a year of unemployment with no disability income, no Voc.Rehab. program, no job training, just aimless job searches before I came upon an opportunity at the Olde and Company stockbrokers firm in downtown Detroit. But I did not mention my records of insanity and incompetence to the personnel managers, and thus I would have severe and traumatic problems later on.

I was laid off in the Winter of 1984 from my trainee position, and I will explain as to the reasons why this occurred in awhile.

In August 1983, I was hired by the personnel managers at Olde and Co., and I was told by my psychiatrists and therapists not to discuss my records of mental incompetency or records of insanity with felony charges psychopathia that I had just diagonally across the street from the stockbrokerage in downtown Detroit. I assumed that the Wayne County chapter of the American Psychiatric Association and the chapter of the American Psychological Association were going to allow the corporation, Olde & Co., to allow me the functions of full licensure there as a broker-dealer trainee. But then came the Winter of 1984, about late January or early February. I was presented by the legal staff and the personnel department with the applications for becoming a rep for the broker-dealer trainee position.

I then told them about my records of incompetency, the records of insanity in the County of Wayne, along with my appeal in process, as well as filling in the entire documents and preparing the filing fees and service fees for the applications. Then I presented the personnel and legal staff with all of the above, and this was early in the week. I expected to be allowed to proceed with the application process, which would lead to more income. I could finally get ready to appeal my case in the appellate levels of courts in the County of Wayne.

But, instead, I was told by the legal staff of Olde & Co., that I would not be allowed to continue as an employee nor trainee of the corporation and that I should have discussed this matter over six months ago with the personnel department. The company was not the Federal Government for my appellate processes, they said, nor were they involved in medical matters. Furthermore, Olde & Co., Inc. could receive tremendous penalties if I was to represent them for full licensure in the present state of my case. Finally, I was told that I should appeal and do the research on my own time and income, and not on company time and company income. I was dismissed, but they told me that I could receive unemployment compensation. My outlook did not look good.

* * *

I then proceeded to go to Florida, which had the lowest unemployment rate in the nation. I was also to receive from Olde & Co., and the State of Michigan, the unemployment benefits I was to apply for in the spring and summer of 1984. I even lived close to the branch offices of Olde & Co., in Fort Lauderdale, Florida.

I had to check into the Federal Job Service Offices and the Florida Employment Security Commission Offices in downtown Fort Lauderdale, Florida. I checked both the private sectors and the public sectors in the area for employment, but to no avail.

A professional recruiter in Fort Lauderdale advised me to pursue the following matter through the locale I was involved with, that is, the area where my disability started. That area being the USA, State of Michigan, County of Wayne, Detroit city area, and to seek housing with my father's permission at home, and to pursue only this item.

Hence, I present:[16]

> But there are programs of direct assistance for the handicapped. Here are the details: Federal Employment

. . .. The Civil Service Commission has selective placement programs to help the handicapped obtain employment with the U.S. government. Included are counseling, referral, placement, and trial appointments. Under the program each federal agency has a coordinator for selective placement, with specific responsibility for assuring that qualified handicapped applicants receive full consideration for employment. To apply for this assistance, handicapped persons should contact the appropriate regional or local office of the Civil Service Commission.

*   *   *

Other Assistance . . . You will be considered for vocational rehabilitation services by your state agency . . . Information in your file is made available to help the specialists in that agency decide whether you can benefit from rehabilitation services and, if so, what kinds of services will be most useful in helping you return to work. (181-2, 192)

With the above knowledge, I then drove back to Michigan from Florida with my dad. He flew to Florida, and we traveled back together to our home in Dearborn Heights. I discussed with him the new-found situation that I was to be involved with in seeking employment and a career, starting in the Detroit area.

In mid-September of 1984, I started the application processes for obtaining employment. I talked with a lady on the phone at the Office of Handicapped Employment for the Federal Government, located in the Federal McNamara Building of downtown Detroit.

She took information by telephone, such as identification, what courts were involved, my psychiatric records as both an inpatient and an outpatient, my Social Security number, etc.

I was told to wait and be called or to call back in about a week from mid-September 1984, this in order to make the initial appointment and the first interview for the program of assistance for the disabled and handicapped in employment opportunities with the Federal Government, on a region to region basis, by the U.S. Civil Service Commission.

But the first interview never occurred.

ENDNOTES CHAPTER 4

1. Document: Savings Account. Savings and Loan, dated August, 1974. Certifies that Caroline Zolkewsky, Successor Trustee, Myron Zolkewsky, Beneficiary. Certificate of deposit of $6,000.00 in the Savings and Loan.
2. Document: General Case Report, Dearborn Heights Police Department, date occurred: 8/30/80. Destruction of Property. Zolkewsky, Alexander as Complainant.
3. Document: State of Michigan, Official Traffic Accident Report, Department Name, Dearborn Heights, Other Complaint No.
4. Documents: State of Michigan, Probate Court for the County of Wayne, in the Matter of legal initials. A. R. Z., or Alexander Robinson Zolkewsky, or in the Matter of legal initials A. Z., or Alexander Zolkewsky, or in the Matter of legal initials A. R., Alex Robinson by File No. . . .; Application for Admission by Medical Certification and Petition for Admission . . . dated November 25, 1980.
5. Document: State of Michigan, Probate Court of the County of Wayne, in the Matter of legal initials A. R. Z, or Alexander Robinson Zolkewsky, or legal initials of A. Z., or Alexander Zolkewsky, or legal initials A. R., Alexander Robinson by File No. . . . Order of Examination and Transport. All three paragraphs. Dated November 25, 1980. Judge of Probate Joseph J. Pernick for Judge of Probate Ernest C. Boehm.
6. Document: Dearborn Heights Police Department. Crime Against Person Case Report . . . Midnight, 12/18/80. Nature of Complaint: Gang Assault and Battery. Complaint Number . . . Complainant Name: Robinson, Alex.
7. Document: Supplementary Report Dearborn Heights Police Department . . . Gang Assault and Battery . . . 12-18-80.
8. Document: Henry Ford Hospital, Fairlane, early morning

Dec. 19, '80 . . . Robinson, Alex.

9. Document: Supplementary Report Dearborn Heights Police Department.

10. Document: Investigation Assault and Battery from Gang . . . dated 3-25-81.

11. Document: Witnesses . . . some data for the records only . . . Officers in Charge of Case . . . Detective Lieutenant with Statements of Defendants.

12. Document: State of Michigan, Crime Victims Compensation Board, Lansing, Michigan, . . . Law Enforcement Agency Verification . . . Section 1 Claim Information . . . Victim . . . Alex Robinson . . . Dearborn Heights . . . Detective Lieutenant . . . dated 4-8-82 . . ..

13. Document: Crime Against Person Case Report, Dearborn Heights Police Department, Gang Assault and Battery. Complaint No. . . . Robinson, Alex . . . Detective Bureau, which is at bottom of page Case Closed in center of page.

14. Document: State of Michigan, Probate Court, County of . . . (blank space) . . . 'this County noted by secondary plaintiff . . . Attorney Anatol Zolkewsky . . . Amended Inventory . . . filed 9-14-81 . . .' 'No primary inventory filed in order to make an amendment inventory during the year of 1981 in Wayne County Court Records . . . this item made by the plaintiff Anatol Zolkewsky . . .' File No. . . . estate of . . . legal initials . . . A. R. Z. . . . or Alexander Robinson Zolkewsky . . .. 'This person supposedly exists by Michigan Driver's License Identification in the County of Wayne . . . as documented by Anatol Zolkewsky . . . I state as defendant that no such person, . . . A. R. Z. . . . does exist by I.D.' Document filed September 14, 1981.

15. Document: Account of Fiduciary, State of Michigan, Probate Court, County if (blank space). This County noted by plaintiff Anatol Zolkewsky. Estate of legal initials A. R. Z. or Alexander Robinson Zolkewsky. Again, this person does not exist by Michigan Driver's License Identification in the County of Wayne, and is stated by plaintiff Anatol Zolkewsky. Guardian: Caroline Zolkewsky: 9-14-81.

16. Document: U.S. News & World Report Money Management Library. *How to Get Your Share of Government*

Treasure: A Guide to Valuable Benefits and Services.

CHAPTER 5

Summary of events near September 28, 1984, concerning the defendant.
Plaintiffs: Individual Officers of the Dearborn Heights Police Department and finally ... Law Student Anatol Zolkewsky

Student Anatol Zolkewsky, plaintiff, affirms and swears to truth of matter, retroactively. The evidence, from the present time and including the last eight years, on entire case history of defendant Alex Robinson, in the Probate Court records in Michigan, County of Wayne.

Also, order processing judge of petition, the "arrest warrant," was the individual officers of the Dearborn Heights Police Department.

Affirmed felony charges, affirmed criminal acts of misconduct are:

1 charge of vandalism,

1 charge of aggravated assault,

1 charge of criminal indirect contempt - whereby the plaintiff, law student Anatol Zolkewsky, affirms to psychiatrists in case testimony, and to all judges in case, that the defendant, Alex Robinson, is ignoring or demeaning a valid court order, won by plaintiffs in Probate Court, County of Wayne, State of Michigan.

This is in reference to the defendant, Alex Robinson, being severely psychotic and ill because of his behavior in 8 years, on record, of being involved in his defendant appeal from probate court orders, back in July, 1976 to the present. The plaintiff, law student Anatol Zolkewsky, affirms that defendant, Alex Robinson, in plaintiff's way presented, is psychotic and ill for trying to base a defense appeal, although this appeal is allowed by law.

The paragraphs above are basically what plaintiff, law student Anatol Zolkewsky, affirmed for the probate court record, County of Wayne, State of Michigan.

Also, plaintiff, law student Anatol Zolkewsky, swears to the truth of matter regarding these facts of the case.

The facts of past record items, decided in judgments by probate court judges, these facts contributing to a psychiatrist's full diagnosis in probate court, of defendant, Alex Robinson, in being severely psychopathic in behavior, with diagnosis on the record.

Plaintiff, law student Anatol Zolkewsky, with Dearborn Heights Police Department individual officers, agree and affirm to past data and information on entire record of case of Alex Robinson, defendant, in his probate court matters, since July, 1976.

Hence, I present:[1]

" I, Anatol Zolkewsky, an adult . . . make this petition/application."

"This conclusion is based upon: (a) My personal observation of the person doing the following acts and saying the following things: 2. Rapid talk about an appeal of a prior commitment to hospital." Here is documented the charge of criminal indirect contempt of court orders upon the defendant by the Dearborn Heights Police Department individual officers and the plaintiff, law student Anatol Zolkewsky. "3 . . . care from Project Paradigm, Ford Rd., Dearborn Heights."

His statement continues: "He attacked Anatol while Anatol was locked in the bedroom." Here is the affirmation of the charge of aggravated assault. "He tried to force the door open." This affirmation is added to the data stated on the trial transcripts involving the charge of vandalism of property, which will be presented. "I therefore request that the subject of this petition be determined by the court to be a person requiring treatment and that until the hearing the individual be hospitalized."

"I declare under penalty of contempt of court that this petition has been examined by me and that its contents are true to the best of my information, knowledge and belief . . . dated September 20, 1984 . . . Signature Anatol Zolkewsky, Dearborn

Heights, Michigan." This petition is accompanied by no checks in any of the following areas: Certificate of Physician, Certificate of Psychiatrist, or Petition for Examination. None of these areas were checked by the plaintiffs, law student Anatol Zolkewsky, nor individual officers of the Dearborn Heights Police Department.

These lies led to the following statement on my Physician's Certificate:[2]

"Likelihood of injury to others. Facts: . . . By report: . . . He physically attacked family members. . . . I therefore conclude that the individual is a person requiring treatment or that the individual is an individual who meets the criteria for judicial admission."

Anatol filed for the following petition:[3]

"Take Notice: On September 28,1984 at . . . in probate courtroom . . . City County Building, Detroit, Michigan, before Hon. Joseph J. Pernick, Judge of Probate . . . a hearing will be held on a petition filed in this court alleging that said person is mentally ill and praying that he may be admitted to some suitable hospital or institution in the State of Michigan for treatment and care."

From the above documents, I state that the plaintiffs, the individual officers of the Dearborn Heights Police Department and law student Anatol Zolkewsky, are creating false charges of vandalism, false charges of aggravated assault, and false charges of criminal indirect contempt. The plaintiffs are committing PERJURY, FRAUD, and CONTEMPT OF COURT upon the Judges, the Courts, the doctors, and several government-mandated offices involved in this case. These lies prevent me from obtaining employment.

"Carry That Weight," <u>Abbey Road</u>, The Beatles.

On September 28, 1984, R. Horvath was appointed the attorney for my Mental Competency Hearing. This hearing went as follows:[4]

Direct Examination:

[Wayne County Prosecutor]: Your name?

Anatol Zolkewsky: Anatol Zolkewsky.

[Wayne County Prosecutor]: And your relationship to Alex Robinson?

Anatol Zolkewsky: I am his brother.

[Wayne County Prosecutor]: Will you tell us the things that occurred, to your personal knowledge, that led you to have to file this petition on September 20, 1984?

Anatol Zolkewsky: On the evening of September 20th . . . he stared banging on the door and he tried to break the lock . . . and he repeated several, several times he was going to kill me . . .. The main reason I petitioned was the fact he was banging the door very hard and I believed that I was in danger.

[Wayne County Prosecutor]: Has your brother had a prior history of psychiatric problems like this?

Anatol Zolkewsky: Yes, he had been committed to a hospital twice . . .. Once in 1974, and another time in 1976. He had been under outpatient treatment since that time. In April of 1984 he moved to Florida, so he wasn't under any family supervision. And he . . . was an entirely different personality. He was extremely detached from the family.

Cross Examination:
[Mr. Horvath]: Mr. Zolkewsky, you indicated that no follow-up treatment as a patient?

Anatol Zolkewsky: Yes.

[Mr. Horvath]: When he wasn't in Florida he stayed at the family residence?
Anatol Zolkewsky: Not the entire time. He had been at Project Paradigm for probably since 1978.

[Mr. Horvath]: He had been doing quite well on the outpatient program, is that right?

Anatol Zolkewsky: He had been non-violent on the outpatient program, but he had not been well. His problems at that time were constant taking of naps. And he was not a problem for anybody, but he was for my mother and grandmother.

[Mr. Horvath]: He never made threats?

Anatol Zolkewsky: Not any violence or abusive problems . . . no . . . he was just extremely docile and somber-like.

[Mr. Horvath]: And you said he went to Florida in April of this year?

Anatol Zolkewsky: Yes.

[Mr. Horvath]: Do you know why?

Anatol Zolkewsky: To find employment.

[Mr. Horvath]: Did anyone try to disillusion him of this?

Anatol Zolkewsky: Not at all . . .. He had managed to complete his bachelor's degree in 1982 in business.

[Mr. Horvath]: Where from?

Anatol Zolkewsky: Madonna College.

[Mr. Horvath]: While he was on the outpatient program?

Anatol Zolkewsky: Yes.

[Mr. Horvath]: He got back in town the 14th of September?

Anatol Zolkewsky: That is correct.

[Mr. Horvath]: And you filed this petition on September 20th?

Anatol Zolkewsky: That is correct.

[Mr. Horvath]: Do you feel if he continued on an outpatient program that he would be able to function as he was doing prior to going to Florida?

Anatol Zolkewsky: His condition, when he returned from Florida, was not at all like it was before he left. It was similar to 1976.

Dr. Smiley Emoni, having been first duly sworn by the Court Clerk to testify, testified as follows:

[Wayne County Prosecutor]: Smiley Emoni . . . licensed to practice medicine in the State of Michigan . . . Is he suffering from a mental illness?

Dr. Emoni: Yes.

[Wayne County Prosecutor]: What is his diagnosis? What are the symptoms of his illness?

Dr. Emoni: He said his brother attacked him because he came back from Florida. Also, he mentioned another reason for his brother's hostility. He said that his brother is the plaintiff and the patient is the defendant about having . . . and also he said that he was trying to defend himself . . . That he was attacked . . . And you heard his brother testify as to his prior history.

[Wayne County Prosecutor]: Is there anything you can add to that?

Dr. Emoni: Yes, there are two previous admissions . . . And I have to add one more thing, that there has been an ongoing family conflict.

[Wayne County Prosecutor]: It appears that this gentleman is at least able to take care of his basic needs, is that correct?

Dr. Emoni: I believe that is correct.

[Wayne County Prosecutor]: Was he willing to sign a consent to treatment?

Dr. Emoni: Yes.

Cross Examination:
[Mr. Horvath]: Doctor, you heard the brother's testimony this morning?

Dr. Emoni: Yes.

[Mr. Horvath]: And he indicated that the respondent

had been able to function pretty well on an outpatient program and that he was able to go to college. Isn't this a good indication for outpatient treatment now?

Dr. Emoni: If he could be released to another program then the problems that arise as a result of the family setting could be avoided.

[Mr. Horvath]: If that would be possible?

Dr. Emoni: I don't know . . . He was living in Florida and these problems occurred.

Alex Robinson, having been first duly sworn by the Court Clerk to testify, testified as follows:

Direct Examination:
[Wayne County Prosecutor]: Please state your name for the record.

Alex Robinson: Alex Robinson.

[Wayne County Prosecutor]: And you are presently at Northville State Hospital, is that correct?

Alex Robinson: Yes, since early in the morning of September 20, 1984 . . .. For approximately six months, I had lived in the Fort Lauderdale, Florida area.

[Wayne County Prosecutor]: Why did you go down to Florida?

Alex Robinson: Upon advice of Project Paradigm, Paradigm Incorporated in Dearborn Heights, Michigan. And my father, Mr. Alexander Zolkewsky, head of household and title holder for the property of the estate. They both recommended that I go in my 13-year-old jalopy from Michigan to Florida to the lowest unemployment rate in the nation to seek employment.

[Wayne County Prosecutor]: Were you successful in getting employment?

Alex Robinson: In approximately six months, the answer is no.

[Wayne County Prosecutor:] Why did you return to Michigan?

Alex Robinson: My father had agreed by telephone that he would fly down from Detroit Metro Airport from point A to point B, Fort Lauderdale, International Airport . . . And we drove back from Florida to Michigan in my 13-year-old jalopy . . . to seek employment in the Michigan area . . . . The Detroit, Michigan area . . . and also specifically to further collect my unemployment compensation through the Michigan Employment Security Commission . . . . I had come in early morning . . . It was September 20, 1984. And I come in the house and the television was on and the lights were on and my brother, Anatol Zolkewsky was standing, watching television, about a half a yard from the television. And I felt immediately that that was strange because somebody that late in early morning from the prior evening would be sitting down, relaxed on the couch watching television, watching television with the lights on . . . Not standing a half a yard away from the television . . . he started screaming, ranting and raving at me. And I just protected myself. He started screaming at me and then he quickly ran to his bedroom and locked the door. And my mother was there and she telephoned the Dearborn Heights Police . . . . Well, first of all I did not threaten him physically or verbally or otherwise to murder him over the last eight years as he stated in the transcript. I say that is a false statement . . . . And also when he was in the bedroom and my mother was on his private phone, calling somebody, because I did not know exactly who she was talking to at the time . . . Answer your question, I have been under court order approximately eight years ago and six years ago to a Project Paradigm . . . P-a-r-a-d-I-g-m. Incorporated, Dearborn Heights, Michigan, where I had been an outpatient with psycho-trophic drugs, psychiatric evaluation, and psychological evaluation as well . . . .

In answering your questions, I do not feel that I should be placed a ninth or tenth day because it is already the eighth day of inpatient treatment at a psychiatric hospital located in Northville, Michigan.

I pray . . . be dismissed to marshall custody . . . father Mr. Alexander Zolkewsky . . . marshall custody . . . dismissed today . . . pastor Mr. John Lazar . . . to our parish in Dearborn Heights, Michigan at the rectory to straighten out my life.

Cross Examination:
[Mr. Horvath]: You heard the doctor testify . . .

Alex Robinson: On the consent agreement form that I signed for Dr. Cha, [phonetic spelling] at the Northville Regional Psychiatric Hospital, I consented and agreed to take psycho-trophic medication. But Dr. Cha, or the document stated because of my emotional problems, I don't feel I have a severe psychotic type of problem to be an inpatient.

[Mr. Horvath]: Do you feel you have enough of a mental problem that you would be willing to take medication on an outpatient basis and follow the direction of the psychiatrist?

Alex Robinson: From today, yes.

[The Court]: This petition will be granted as prayed .

. . That will be all, Mr. Robinson.

From the above given data, documents, and transcripts, I state that there is false testimony from the plaintiff, law student Anatol Zolkewsky. On the evening testified I was incarcerated from the early morning in the County of Wayne, NRPH, and I will present documents to show that I did not do the above psychopathia on the evening of 9-20-84 while placed in NRPH. The doctors' records show that I did not do the stated actions. Nor did I do the psychotic actions any other evening. I state that there is no Dearborn Heights Emergency Medical Services Ambulance unit evidence, nor is there any Emergency Room evidence of any damages of an aggravated assault upon the plaintiff from the ER of any hospital the three nights specifically in question.

Also, I state that there is no evidence of a Dearborn Heights Police report, locksmith reports of repairs, or insurance payments to dad for property damages of door.

The plaintiff, law student Anatol Zolkewsky, affirms that I tried to break the door down. I, the defendant, state that there is no evidence, nor was there ever any evidence, of the charges of vandalism in my dad's house during the week of the mid-September period of time in the records of the case.

The plaintiffs have committed PERJURY, CONTEMPT OF COURT, and FRAUD upon the Judges, the Courts, the doctors, and several government-mandated offices involved in this case. And the plaintiffs chose to do the above on their own accord and their own actions of choice, for the records.

Next I show:[5]

Section, Contempt . . . Criminal contempt . . . is an act that violates the dignity of a court or its processes . . . Acts constituting contempt of court include . . . obstructing justice, disobeying a court order . . ..

Indirect contempt is contempt outside the courtroom: a violation of a court order . . ..

Section, Perjury . . . to give false testimony in court . . . If in a judicial proceeding someone willfully gives false testimony or information under oath, in matters material to the issue involved, he has committed the offense of perjury . . . Although perjury is most often associated with judicial proceedings, you should take care not to perjure yourself -- knowingly make material false statements.

I present this to clarify my position and the wrong actions of all plaintiffs involved in this case. They have created a distortion of so-called facts. The plaintiffs, all of them, have had ten complete years to step forward and to make confessions and restitution to the defendant in the case with defense counsel and the judges. But this has not occurred.

Note that my discharge report from November 16, 1984, states that I had "no behavior problems."

Also, look at Dr. Adam's treatment notes:

He was brought to Hegira by the Dearborn Heights Police Department. He was dressed appropriately . . . He states, he has been found guilty of . . . felony charges as regards to being mentally ill . . . Client denies being homicidal, denies all statements made in the petition. He states, he can't work for 40 years because of his felony conviction . . . No such convictions exist . . ..

The patient was evaluated by myself at Northville Regional Psychiatric Hospital . . . He did give responses to questions. When asked if he had a psychiatric problem, he responded, "I don't feel I am psychopathic, I don't have V.D., I have an emotional problem . . . I request to go to Project Paradigm where I have been going for six years." . . . He further stated, "I refuse to go to a court hearing . . . eight years ago, the judge laughed at me and condemned me . . .. When discussing the judge, he stated, "The judge can insert . . . (cellulose) . . . and inorganic ink in my file, then, I can continue to get my life together."

*   *   *

Mental Status Examination: General Disposition: He did

accompany me to the interview room without incident. Speech and motor: There is gross pressured speech and motor restlessness evident throughout the interview. Mood and Affect: There was no evidence of depression.

Thought Content: . . . The patient appeared oriented to time, place, and person. There was no gross hallucinations elicited. The patient denied hearing voices. His memory was intact. His intelligence was average. His sensorium was clear at this time.

Psycho-Dynamic Formulation: This 30-year-old, white, single male went to Florida, where he was basically on unemployment compensation and other forms of state aide for approximately half a year. He returned to Michigan five days prior to this admission . . . He has been without medications.

Prognosis: It is anticipated that he will be stabilized with chemotherapy and again be released to the community.

I wrote a letter to Project Paradigm, requesting all my psychiatric records from August, 1978 to April, 1984, but I was presented with a booklet entitled, "Reach for a Better Life." On the back it read, "You don't have to be alone."

I was told by staff and employees that my outpatient records in the County of Wayne, State of Michigan, were classified and as such, I was not allowed to obtain even a basic summary report of my stated compliance, outlook, diagnosis and prognosis, evaluation, or any other reports.

All of the above would have been made in a report by the psychiatric clinic, and I could have paid for the necessary service fees involved.

I commented that anybody could have received my court records and my inpatient records in the County of Wayne, State of Michigan. But I did not understand the situation that was presented above, for I was told that I would need a judge's and court order to simply obtain a summary of my outpatient treatment at Project Paradigm, Inc. over the last eight years.

So that is why I must present the minimum evidence of my

outpatient psychiatric clinic therapy and proper treatment. It should be very helpful in combating the plaintiffs in this case with their lying on records in the County of Wayne, State of Michigan.

I will show the proper diagnosis and proper treatment shortly, these items pertaining to this case. It seems the doctors recently in my case have completely disregarded and have not believed any of the data so far presented in this case over the last ten years of accumulated data and records of my case.

I state that my diagnosis should be severe depression and schizophrenia, which it is now, and that it should be based on none of the psychosis, none of the psychopathia affirmed by all the plaintiffs in this case over the last decade. My problems could have been handled through my pastor of the church of our religious faith, my Ukrainian Catholic Church located in Dearborn Heights. My depression problems could have been handled through Father John Lazar, by having him refer me to the proper doctors, counselors, and therapists. I would have had private medical insurance to pay the costs of my treatment. The treatment would have been the result of my observed and acknowledged behavior regarding severe depression, this resulting from the parents, the disharmony of my family environment, the neglect of the parents upon me and the "broken home" situation.

I state that the plaintiffs living at my house at 8090 Dale St. in Dearborn Heights are lying to the courts, lying to the judges, and lying to the doctors. And I allowed them a full ten years of time, in order for them to make confessions to the above authorities, in order to set the record straight, to state what is really occurring and what has occurred in the past.

But none of the plaintiffs have stepped forward and made confessions to the truth that I, as the defendant, must now bring forward to this appellate court. I state that I have told the truth all along, did not do the affirmed psychopathia nor the affirmed psychotic actions on the case record, and I feel that I have proven that.

I have taken Pamelor and Stelazine, which were prescribed to me as therapy for severe depression and schizophrenia. They make me feel much better about myself. I took these medicines along with good dosages of aspirin, usually 1,000 milligrams, whenever headaches occurred in this hateful environment for the last ten to fifteen years.

I state that the medicines that I had to ingest in the last ten years, all the psycho tropics, all the tranquilizers, and all the depressants in my system just seemed to continue my problems with depression in the first place. Over the past one year, having the proper medicines, anti-depressants, in me, that I am elevating myself to be a better person.

Next I present:[6]

"Mother . . . noun . . .3.: maternal tenderness of affection" and

"Motherhood . . . noun . . . the state of being a mother." also

"Wife . . . noun . . . 1b.: a woman acting in a specified capacity . . . 2.: a married woman." and

"Wifehood . . . noun . . . the quality or state of being a wife."

From the above definitions presented, I state that this Caroline, whatever her last name, does not fit the definitions, nor has she fit these definitions in the last 20 years. She has not fulfilled these definitions especially in the last ten years, involving the time period of this case.

"Yer Blues," The Beatles (White Album), The Beatles.

I state for the record that she, Caroline, did commit acts of PERJURY, CONTEMPT OF COURT, and FRAUD upon the Judges, the Courts, the doctors, and several government-mandated offices in this case. She lied to the above in the capacity of a wife and a mother in the County of Wayne, State of Michigan. She was also given a period of ten years to make confessions and restitution to the defendant, Alex Robinson, and even to the victim-plaintiff, Alexander Zolkewsky, as well.

This father of mine went to invest thousands of dollars in black markets behind the Iron Curtain and in Poland, starting in 1968, then in 1970, 1972, 1974, 1976, 1978, 1980, and 1984. He pulled away about $3,000 each visit, multiplied by his eight visits or about a sum total of $24,000 that he removed from our little existence.

He kept telling me that he was helping himself and our family in America. He was taking a vacation from his wife and my mother. I asked to see Federal Income Tax documents and verification of this supposed helping of the family, but he always refused. We would be termed a low-income household, but a blue-collar income household, a working-class and middle-income level of household for economic analysis, as we needed every penny for sound economics and financial strength.

My chances for a future have been shattered.

Hence, I ask and pray that these appellate court judges in this case state and court order the victim-plaintiff, Alexander Zolkewsky, this dad of mine, to produce the following Federal Income Tax Documents in order to show that he is supposedly helping the family in the USA by many deductions in the thousands of dollars and income tax credits in the hundreds of dollars here in America.

I state that he cannot produce anything of helpfulness, and these areas are a source of never-ending hostility between Alexander Zolkewsky and Caroline Zolkewsky ... and between the father and his eldest son, the defendant, Alex Robinson, in the case.

I hope and pray that my dad can show the court and me, the defendant, income tax proof, pertaining to the long-running family argument that has raged on for the last 20 years.

I state that he cannot show anything of the above and that he was wrong to continue for the last 20 years.

Finally, I present this document:[7]

"Per your letter of May 2, 1986, I am closing my files ... A lawsuit has not been instituted at this time ... Therefore, if in the future you should decide to change your mind and initiate a lawsuit against the physicians involved in your case, ... I respect your decision not to go forward in the case ... Sincerely, Jeffrey T. Meyers."

I show this letter as evidence to state that the doctors were simply lied to by the plaintiffs and the police in this case in the County of Wayne, State of Michigan. I state that the doctors are not at fault, but it is the plaintiffs who are completely at fault in this case.

ENDNOTES CHAPTER 5

1. Document: Petition/Application for Hospitalization, State of Michigan, Probate Court, County of . . . (blank space) . . . in the Matter of Alex Robinson. Judge: Joseph J. Pernick, File: September 21, 1984. Deputy Probate Register. File No. . . .

2. Document: Physician's Certificate, State of Michigan, Probate Court, County of . . . (blank space) . . . in the Matter of Alex Robinson.

3. Document: Notice of Hearing, State of Michigan, Probate Court, Wayne County, File No. . . . in the Matter of Alex Robinson . . . to Anatol Zolkewsky.

4. Document: State of Michigan, in the Probate Court for the County of Wayne, in the Matter of the Estate of: Alex Robinson . . . File No. Mental Competency Hearing before the Honorable Frank S. Szymanski - Judge . . . Friday, September 28, 1984 - Detroit, Michigan.

5. Document: You and the Law, Reader's Digest, Henry Ford Centennial Library, Dearborn, Michigan.

6. Document: Webster's Seventh New Collegiate Dictionary . . . Page 553 and 1020.

7. Document: Law Offices of Chambers, Steiner, Mazur, Ornstein & Amlin, P.C. Detroit. Jeffrey T. Meyers. Heading to Mr. Alex Robinson, dated June 16, 1986.

CHAPTER 6

I will now proceed with my closing summary defense statements on this case, as the defendant, Alex Robinson, in the County of Wayne, State of Michigan.

Since I was incarcerated in the mental hospital by the plaintiffs and the police, I feel I should comment on what I observed. It seems that I was hated severely by my status as a person, as an American. The plaintiffs show a complete hatred towards me and my father, both on college transcript records and in my appearance and correlated work to have my appearance as presented. The plaintiffs stated and prayed that I should be placed in the mental patient status, the lower-lower class status, as provided by laws and statutes. The plaintiffs placed me in the status of mental incompetence, with a basis of record of insanity with felony charges psychosis, or the acts of criminal misconduct along with the formal records. They seemed to do this as a group tactic, as a group or gang policy towards the establishment of case family law, since I am told that probate court deals in this realm.

"While my Guitar Gently Weeps," The Beatles (White Album), The Beatles.

The plaintiffs falsified data in order to establish rules and regulations by acts of state legislature in an errant pattern. They also falsified data to the Federal Congress where federal lawmakers also were led astray in any matters dealing with case laws and family laws and patterns of public policy applied to constitutional rights and individuals, here in the USA.

While incarcerated in the mental hospital, falsely as proven, I observed that I was locked up with U.S. Armed Forces personnel with the labeling and status of a Vietnam Veteran.

I was shocked at this situation, American military veterans, 11 year Vietnam Veterans in the USA, were simply incarcerated in the mental hospital. I observed that they had a direct correlation with my case in that there was no evidence, no substantial evidence, nor reasons for them to be incarcerated other than the pure hatred of them as military veterans on American soil. In nice discussion with several of them, I came to this conclusion.

The Vietnam Veterans that I was incarcerated with in July, 1976, for example, said that they would have their cases proven to be directly correlated with PERJURY, CONTEMPT OF COURT, and FRAUD upon them as well as proven in my own separate case in jurisdiction of the courts in the County of Wayne, State of Michigan.

But I am not their U.S. Armed Forces military lawyer to set the record straight on matters of having a nice status such as an American military veteran with good benefits in the USA, as well as myself in being a college weight lifter whom I claimed that the plaintiffs and the police in my own case were hateful liars towards me, pertaining to the USA Constitution and individual rights correlated with American citizenship rights.

For my own case, the plaintiffs showed how reckless they were in lying. I have shown that they, the plaintiffs in this case, have falsified data and falsely affirmed items and actions, which did not occur. As to the reasons for their actions, I cannot explain why, but simply will prove that they lied to the Judges, the Courts, the doctors, and they lied to several government-mandated offices involved in the case. I state that they should explain why they lied to both the local and county authorities as well as why they lied to Federal authorities.

"Sgt. Pepper's Lonely Hearts Club Band (Reprise)" and "A Day in the Life,"
<u>Sgt. Pepper's Lonely Hearts Club Band</u>, The Beatles.

In conclusion:
The plaintiff, Caroline Zolkewsky, has committed PERJURY, CONTEMPT OF COURT and FRAUD upon the

defendant, Alex Robinson, and items documented in this case.

The plaintiff, Caroline Zolkewsky, committed PERJURY, CONTEMPT OF COURT and FRAUD on the following amounts of felony charges psychosis, of amounts of charges of criminal acts of misconduct on this case.

11 charges of PERJURY and CONTEMPT OF COURT, these upon the defendant.

They are as follows: Three charges of assault and battery, three charges of reckless driving, two charges of vandalism, one charge of larceny of mail, one charge of larceny of money, and one charge of assault and battery.

Also;

The plaintiff, Caroline Zolkewsky, committed FRAUD against the following: Michigan Department of Mental Health, Social Security Administration, Medicare, Michigan Department of Education Bureau of Rehabilitation, Internal Revenue Service, Michigan Department of Treasury, Our Lady of Perpetual Help, and the Ukrainian Catholic Church.

And;

The plaintiff, Myron Zolkewsky, Private Investigator and Corporation, has committed PERJURY and CONTEMPT OF COURT upon the defendant, Alex Robinson, and items documented in this case.

The plaintiff, Myron Zolkewsky, committed PERJURY and CONTEMPT OF COURT on the following amounts of felony charges psychosis, of amounts of charges of criminal acts of misconduct on this case.

11 charges of PERJURY and CONTEMPT OF COURT, these upon the defendant.

They are as follows: Three charges of assault and battery, three charges of reckless driving, two charges of vandalism, one charge of larceny of mail, one charge of larceny of money, and one charge of assault and battery.

Also;

The plaintiff, Myron Zolkewsky, committed FRAUD against the following: Michigan Department of Mental Health, Social Security Administration, Medicare, Michigan Department of Education Bureau of Rehabilitation, Interanl Revenue Service,

Michigan Department of Treasury, Our Lady of Perpetual Help, and the Ukrainian Catholic Church.

Furthermore;

The plaintiff, Anatol Zolkewsky, Attorney at Law, has committed PERJURY and CONTEMPT OF COURT upon the defendant, Alex Robinson, and items documented in this case.

The plaintiff, Aanatol Zolkewsky, committed PERJURY and CONTEMPT OF COURT on the following amounts of felony charges psychosis, of amounts of charges of criminal acts of misconduct on this case.

14 charges of PERJURY and CONTEMPT OF COURT, these upon the defendant.

They are as follows: Three charges of assault and battery, three charges of reckless driving, two charges of vandalism, one charge of larceny of mail, one charge of larceny of money, one charge of assault and battery, one charge of vandalism, one charge of aggravated assault and one charge of indirect criminal contempt.

Also;

The plaintiff, Anatol Zolkewsky, committed FRAUD against the following: Michigan Department of Mental Health, Social Security Administration, Medicare, Michigan Department of Education Bureau of Rehabilitation, Interanl Revenue Service, Michigan Department of Treasury, Our Lady of Perpetual Help, and the Ukrainian Catholic Church.

In summation, I state that I pray and hope for removal, reversal, further consideration of, and request that on my appeal to these courts and judges, that I win as a defendant in dismissing the lower court, the probate court orders, that have been placed upon me for the last ten years and will affect me for the rest of my lifetime. I claim PERJURY, CONTEMPT OF COURT and FRAUD by the plaintiffs in this case, as well as by the individual officers of the Dearborn Heights Police Department.

I close my appellate court statement as of now.

Thank you, Your Honor.

About the Author

The author graduated from Dearborn Fordson H.S., 1972. He accepted a work-study program at Mich. State Univ. in a hospital and studied pre-medicine from 1972-1975. In 1977-'79 he worked in pre-business studies at Wayne St. Univ. in Detroit, from which he was stopped by police. He attended Madonna Univ. in Livonia, MI from 1979-July '82. He graduated with a B.S. in Banking and has worked as a Medic, worked nights as an orderly, broker clerk and guard. After college he weightlifted in weight rooms for 5 years to relieve stress caused by this case.

www.ingramcontent.com/pod-product-compliance
Lightning Source LLC
Chambersburg PA
CBHW030838180526
45163CB00004B/1372